"A KINGDOM WHICH CANNOT BE SHAKEN"

Overcoming in the Midst of Chaos

ROBERT FARRIER

Printed in the United States of America

Published by Bob Farrier Ministries

Unless otherwise indicated, all Scripture quotations are from *The Holy Bible, New King James Version.* © Copyright 1982 by Thomas Nelson, Inc. Used by permission.

ISBN- 13: 978-0615470818
ISBN- 10: 0615470815

For additional copies, you can order from Publisher at www.kingdomfaithconnection.com or www.createspace.com/3579780

Special Acknowledgement

I would like to give acknowledgement and special thanks to the following people who helped make this book possible: Rev. James Jones, Assistant Missions Professor, at Southeastern University, Lakeland, Fl, who in 1978 first opened my eyes regarding the Grand Plan that God has for us in His Kingdom; the late Dr. Clarence E. Fast, Pastor and friend who first taught me how to be sensitive to the leading of the Spirit of God; and to Dr. Chad and Katie Bardsley, who having endured two teaching sessions of this material, inspired and encouraged the turning of my notes into the writing of this book.

"And I, brethren, when I came to you, did not come with excellence of speech or wisdom declaring to you the testimony of God. For I determied not to know anything among you except Jesus Christ and Him crucified. I was with you in weakness, in fear, and in much trembling. And my speech and my preaching were not with persuasive words of human wisdom, but in the demonstration of the Spirit and of power, that your faith should not be in the wisdom of men but in the power of God"

1 Cor 2:1-5 NKJV

Contents

Preface

Jesus, when He had finished giving the Beatitudes, wasted no time in letting His followers know what to expect if they continued with Him. They could expect to be despised, mistreated and have all kinds of evil falsely said against them. They could expect to be counted with the prophets of old who were persecuted and killed; in that, they were to rejoice.

On the Mount of Transfiguration, the Father opened the heart of Peter, James and John when He said, *"This is My Son in whom I am well pleased, hear Him"*. They recognized who Jesus truly was, not only their Savior but also their King. Therefore, these early Apostles and Disciples were willing to die for their faith and many of them did. Their commitment to Jesus Christ was because of their perception of who He was; the Lord of Glory, the Prince of Peace, the King of Kings and Lord of lords.

They understood that Jesus had come to Earth to reclaim His Father's Kingdom. They understood that He had formed and empowered His Church to use His name to extend His Kingdom throughout the whole Earth.

The power and authority given to the Church enabled it, as the Body of Christ, to go forth and engage in spiritual warfare. This power and authority foreshadowed the central function in their purpose. Jesus said that He would build His Church and the gates of hell would not prevail against it. That phrase, "prevail against it", tells the story of the future battles for the Church and the victory to follow.

The early Church experienced persecution for several reasons including the following: a simplistic lifestyle that looked to the immediate needs of their fellow Christians while exhorting one another to be gainfully employed; not be idle or looking to the state for help. Christians were viewed as separatist because their moral standards were seen as a severe reproach to the pagan way of life, and they were described as unique in their attitude toward persecution, their devotion to family and to their God. Their generosity to the poor, their love for their enemies, their humility, their mercy toward the repentant, and their love for righteousness distinguished them from all others.

The problems multiplied for those that converted to Christianity because of the way in which they broke from the social norms of their surrounding society. The Church, "the called out ones", began to reflect a new culture that caused them to withdraw from the social, political and economic structures in place. They began to reflect the culture of the Kingdom of God, which is in direct opposition to the culture of the world.

Most importantly, it was their message of a new Kingdom reserved for those who committed their life to Christ Jesus, the Jewish Messiah that angered the Jews and the Romans alike. Because of their allegiance to their Savior King, there hung a question mark over their loyalty to the State. It is possible that Christians suffered not so much for their doctrinal differences of faith from the Romans but rather for their avowed allegiance to a Heavenly throne and its Law. These early Christians did not offer worship to the pagan throne nor to the State; this was interpreted as treason and disloyalty.

If we, the Church of the 21st Century, recapture a Kingdom Mindset and then begin to live out a Kingdom Culture, we will suffer persecution for the same reasons. We are not talking of the distant future but the immediate present. The Church is already finding itself in the crosshairs of an ever-increasing secular humanistic society; a society that says it no longer needs the guidance and assistance of an almighty God, in fact, a God in which it no longer believes.

We are already facing the evils of a godless society as those in power thrust their desires upon us through secular laws, music, arts, education, government policies, and false religion. Those with a platform are using their voice to say what many in America are already thinking – Christians are dangerous. Many believe that Christians are no different from any other religious fanatics, such as the militant jihadists using their religion as a front to battle against the majority and the right of reason. They view anyone who takes the Bible seriously, believes in the literal meaning of the 10 commandments or takes a stand against abortion and gay marriage as people who are ignorant bigots, degenerates or America's equivalent of suicide bombers.

Because America is the last stronghold of any resemblance of Kingdom Culture in the world, the forces of Darkness are attacking vigorously. On every front of our American culture, we are experiencing an enemy offense being waged against us. There is a battle going on in America. It is not Republicans or Conservatives versus the Democrats. It is spiritual battle of secular humanism and the Church of the Lord Jesus Christ.

The Church must take the blame for the evil condition of our society because it failed to "pass the baton" on to the next generations that were in positions of leadership. Just in the last 70 years, we have seen with each of the last four generations the numbers of people holding to Bible-based values decline from **65%** in my generation (BUILDERS) (1924-1945) to **35%** in the next (BOOMERS) (1946 -1964) down to **16%** in the next (BUSTERS) (1965-1983) then dropping dramatically to **4%** for the present generation (Generation X'ERS). How low will it go?

Is there any wonder that morality is at an all time low here in America. Is it any wonder that the younger generation cannot discern right from wrong? Eighty-five percent (85%) of teenagers think morals are relative, only 6% believe in absolute truth and tragically, only 9% of "Born-Again" teenagers believe in absolute truth as revealed in the Bible. Because the divorce rate has reached an all time high along with a corresponding increase for those that publicly support homosexuality; the assault on American families is as great has it has ever been.

The wholesale acceptance of Science contributes to the battle, as our children believe Evolution as a fact instead as a disproven theory. Our children's History textbooks have been changed so that they have no real basis for decision making for the future.

In the last few years, it seems like a cultural broom is sweeping across the world, especially America, to brush

7

Christianity into a godless pit allowing Materialism and Humanism to reign in the hearts of men and women. The Worldviews of those we held in esteem are now being exposed to be filled with deceit and self-serving intentions.

However, it is not too late! The world has not seen the last of Jesus Christ. It is not the physical person of Jesus Christ that I'm talking about, even though He will soon return as King of kings and Lord of lords. What I'm talking about is the Church of the Lord Jesus Christ.

The Church is the body of Christ. The same Spirit that empowered Jesus is empowering His Body. Jesus said, *"Most assuredly, I say to you, he who believes in Me, the works that I do he will do also; and greater works than these he will do, because I go to My Father. And whatever you ask in My name, that I will do, that the Father may be glorified in the Son. If you ask anything in My name, I will do. John 14:12-14*

In our first book, *BORN TO RULE*, we said the one behind the scene, who is manipulating the rich and powerful, is non-other than Satan himself. Satan does not need to use guns or weapons of mass destruction; he is far wiser than that. His tool is deceit. He is a master at lying and intrigue. Words are the tools of his craft. He has his men and women who will listen to him and do his bidding, thinking that they will receive honor and glory for themselves when, in truth, Satan is just using them to further his kingdom. In the end, they will be discarded like an old worn out pair of shoes.

Christians who are taken in by the lies of materialism are seeking security for their possessions, rather than trusting in a loving God who will be there in the good times and the bad times. We seem to be searching for peace here on Earth through prosperity instead of embracing the Prince of Peace. What is so alarming is that the Church of today has already bought into the deception of materialism. From sermons and books, Christians are learning to accept the Blessings of things as a automatic right. They have been told that Christianity is the way to get rich and the way to becoming a better you. If one is living right, believing right, then Prosperity is a God given right.

Preface

WHAT YOU WILL LEARN IN THE CHAPTERS THAT FOLLOW AND WHAT YOU LEARNED FROM OUR FIRST BOOK WILL BE THE TOOLS IN YOUR HANDS TO WITHSTAND THE LIES AND THE CRAFTINESS OF THE SPIRIT OF ANTICHRIST. THE APOSTLE JOHN TOLD US THAT MANY ANITICHRISTS HAVE ALREADY COME INTO THE WORLD. NEVERTHELESS, WE ARE NOW NEARER TO THE END THEN EVER BEFORE. WE ARE ON THE EDGE OF A WORLDWIDE EXPLOSION OF VIOLENCE IN OUR STREETS. IN THE CITY STREETS ACROSS EUROPE, AFRICA, ASIA AND SOUTH AMERICA, IT IS ALREADY HAPPENING. PRESSURE WILL BE BROUGHT ON THE GOVERNING BODIES ACROSS THE GLOBE TO END THIS VIOLENCE. HYPER- INFLATION IS COMING, BLOODSHED IS COMING, ECONOMIC COLLAPSE IS COMING, SICKNESS AND DISEASE THAT WILL AFFECT MILLIONS IS COMING. WE MUST BE READY.

THE PRINCIPLES FOUND IN THE FOLLOWING PAGES ARE NOT TO HELP YOU ESCAPE BUT TO OVERCOME. GOD WILL USE PERSECUTION TO EXTEND HIS KINGDOM AND WE HAVE THE PRIVILEGE TO BE A PART OF HIS END-TIME HARVEST.

Jesus said, *"But when they arrest you and deliver you up, do not worry beforehand, or premeditate what you will speak. But whatever is given you in that hour, speak that; for it is not you who speak, but the Holy Spirit. Now brother will betray brother to death, and a father his child; and children will rise up against parents and cause them to be put to death. And you will be hated by all for My name's sake. But he who endures to the end shall be saved".* Mark 13:11-13

What a promise to those that endure; we shall be saved. We will receive our inheritance and rule with Christ. The Christ who came to Earth as a child shall one day rule the Earth, *"For unto us a Child is born, unto us a Son is given; and the government will be upon His shoulder. And His name will be called Wonderful, Counselor, Mighty God, Everlasting Father, Prince of Peace. Of the increase of His government and peace there will be no end, upon the throne of David and over His kingdom, to order it and establish it with judgment and justice from that time forward, even forever. The zeal of the Lord of hosts will perform this".*

For the last fifteen years, I have been proclaiming to the Nations our need to grow our faith, for the time is coming soon when God will shake both the Heavens and the Earth. The time is now for us to mature in our faith, work the "works of God", and make His name known to all the Nations.

Our prayer for you is that the Kingdom of God will expand because of your acquiring a heart for ministry. We desire that you will have birthed within you a heart that will carry the truth of God's love to those in need, and that the power of God will flow out through you like a stream of fresh water.

Bob Farrier

Introduction

Dr. Lloyd Ogilive, retired Chaplin of the US Senate, started his book, DRUMBEAT OF LOVE, with these words: "Everywhere I go these days I hear the same urgent appeal from Christians. They want their lives to count. Their greatest fear is that they might live their lives in ineffectiveness, ineptness, or insipidness. They long for a challenge *big enough* to demand their allegiance, *exciting enough* to rally their enthusiasm and *crucial enough* to warrant their time."

The challenge we will present in this second book will help you in your quest for hearing the voice of the Spirit of God that will lead you on to maturity. John Wesley said; "Give me one hundred men who fear nothing but sin and desire nothing but God, and I care not whether they be clergyman or laymen, they alone will shake the gates of Hell and set up the kingdom of Heaven upon the earth." He was looking for people that were demanding such a challenge. Christ Jesus is looking for people with the same heart today.

On the day of Pentecost, Jesus breathed life into the "called out ones" and the Church was born. The Church began its life with 120 men and women who went out to, "shake the gates of Hell and set up the Kingdom of Heaven upon the earth". Today His Church is calling out to its brothers and sisters, "Awake, awake from your slumber and sleep. Church is not as many think; it is not just about preaching social norms, about the cross of Christ so that others can be saved, live good lives, and then go to heaven when they die. No, it is that and much more. It is no longer the time for "church as usual" because God is saying "Awake" for the time has come."

The first Church was a group of people that gathered together because they had heard the Lord of their life say, *"Come and follow me"*. They heard the call to maturity. They left the crowd and started a walk with Jesus; a walk in which they would come to see life differently and as a result, their transformation process began. They had a desire to receive the promised power in order that they might take the love of God to a dry and thirsty land. They sensed, as we do, that God's timing is now.

LEADING THE WAY

The greatness of a leader is in his/her ability to reproduce themselves in the lives of others. Rosalynn Carter said, "A leader takes people where they want to go. A great leader takes people where they don't necessarily want to go, but ought to go".

Jesus was such a leader on a mission. He was out to change the world. He had only three years to gather followers, transform them into Believers that could represent him and empower them to go into the entire world and extend His kingdom into the lives of people everywhere.

In the first year and a half of his ministry, Jesus revealed who He was. He gave His disciples a vision of His Kingdom and its culture, explained in detail how they were to live in His Kingdom and gave them faith and courage to follow Him. They took up their cross and then lived by the life of another. This we covered in Volume One of this work, *"BORN TO RULE"*.

In the second one and a half years of His ministry, Jesus gave them opportunity to experience for themselves the supernatural ministry of the Holy Spirit. They preached about the Kingdom and the love and grace of God, healed the sick, cast out demons, and brought wholeness to the lives of their fellow citizens. This is what we will now discover in Volume Two, *"A KINGDOM WHICH CANNOT BE SHAKEN"*.

The principles that Jesus utilized in leading them through the process of Empowerment are just as valid today. The Pathway to effective ministry is just as difficult and just as rewarding today, as it was for those 1st Century Disciples.

Maybe you have dreamed of being another Moses or Apostle Paul. You have tried to do something great, only to realize that without God's anointing and the proper preparation you are destined to failure.

After 40 years of preparing Moses for the task of being Israel's deliverer, God brought him to Mount Horeb. There the Angel of God appeared to him in the flame of fire from the midst of a bush. Moses saw the burning bush and wondered why the fire did not consume it. He said, *"I will now turn aside and see why the bush does not burn."* When God saw that Moses turned aside to look at the bush, God spoke to him.

I believe that you, like many Believers, are ready to turn aside to see why the bush is not consumed. You are ready to accept the miraculous and are longing to make the Name of your God known. Having entered the Transformation process, you are now ready to let King Jesus take you aside and Empower you. As Moses went from a retreat and defensive position to one of attack and conquest, you are ready to do the same.

Whatever your calling, *"A KINGDOM WHICH CANNOT BE SHAKEN"* will awaken you to the voice of God so that you will know Him and enable you to be quiet within your spirit so that you can receive revelation of His greatness. It will provide you with a challenge and stir up a vision within your being so that you will give your all to satisfy the hunger to be filled with His presence and therefore be filled with His power.

OUR FOCUS

Many today are still confused as to how to go about the "work of the Ministry". They are so used to just "going" to church that the thought of "being the Church" is a little overwhelming. They have grown however, beyond acceptance of only a pastoral nurturing, bless-me culture. They want to do more than just fill a seat in a sanctuary; they want to be equipped and make a difference in the lives of others and therefore advance the Kingdom of God into areas not yet established.

Jesus said for us to go out into the highways and byways and compel them (be persistent in nagging) to come into the Kingdom. This goes way beyond what the present day church is doing. The church has laid claim to "making Disciples" by stressing "Servant hood". They encourage leaders to be "servant leaders". They encourage others to do those things that answer the question, "WWJD". Its members feel good at the end of the day when they have mowed a yard for an elderly widow, fixed a roof, or made a meal or two for someone just getting home from the hospital.

This is not to belittle them or make light of their giving. The point to be made is this; being an Overcomer goes way, way beyond that. It is a call to "die to self". Dietrich Bonheoffer said it best when he said, "When Christ calls a man, He bids him come and die". We are not all called to martyrdom, as was he, but we are all called to commit ourselves totally to our King; allowing the Holy Spirit to have free access to our lives. The Father's intention is for the Holy Spirit to lead us in whatever endeavors that would prepare and qualify us to participate in His Grand Plan.

People all around you are in need. They are looking for real answers to real problems. As you apply yourself to the principles found in this book, you can meet those needs by the grace given you and the empowerment of the Holy Spirit. You will provide a Word of Knowledge to someone that needs an answer, a Word of Wisdom to someone who seeks direction. You will lay hands on the sick and they will be healed. You will cast out demons and set captives free. Jesus said, *"great works you will do and even greater works because I go to the Father"*. Yes, this means YOU!

You and the people in your Church that are like-minded can start your own outreach to those in need. Yes, go find a need and fill it. Take the Kingdom of God and its life-giving power to those outside the Church walls. Get yourself a "buddy" and both of you go to someone in need of healing. Take what the Holy Spirit has revealed to you through this training and let the presence of the

Holy Spirit bring healing through your touch. That is what Jesus did and that is what He taught His disciples to do.

This book has as its focus to inspire you to answer the call that Jesus brings to you personally and for you to realize that you are part of a family, a family that is called to, "come and die". For it is only in your dying to self that brings life is to others. It is only in your dying to self that the Holy Spirit can flow out from you and bring faith, love and hope to others. It is only in your dying to self that Jesus can live His life through you. To do this you must have Purpose, a Mission and a Vision.

"I WILL BUILD MY CHURCH".

The Church is the gathering place of those that are "called out" from the World. Each Believer has within them the Kingdom of God (the influence, power and authority of God), not just for their lives but also to influence the world around them. Jesus started with twelve disciples and the Kingdom of God began to grow. His disciples grew into thousands. Jewish leaders were being converted. Tax collectors and fishing boat owners were also added to the list and even a Roman centurion came under the influence of the Kingdom of God.

Jesus sent the twelve out and then the seventy; they too preached the Gospel of the Kingdom. More people came into the Kingdom of God and under the influence of God and His authority. The people gathered and a culture was established. Jesus explained the character of the citizens of the Kingdom and then revealed to them the culture of the Kingdom as it was to be displayed in their lives and how they were to relate to those still in the World under the rulership of Satan.

The Church was growing and the world around them was changing. They were affecting the government, the arts, the health system, the economic system, language, religion, traditions and the social organization of the areas where they went.

They were extending the kingdom of God here on Earth. They were literally fulfilling the Prayer that Jesus taught them; *"Thy Kingdom come, on Earth, as it is in heaven"*.

Jesus said that He would build His Church. The Church, however, is not His Kingdom but it is the control center of the Father's Kingdom. The purpose of the Church is to bring God's government and culture to the earth by teaching, explaining, and encouraging people to come into the Kingdom and have a relationship with the King. The Church is to make the mighty name of their King known throughout the world as its members go forth in the power of the Holy Spirit.

In order for this to happen, a change in the style of the Church's leadership must occur. We will soon find the Church doing those things that are maturing and equipping the saints in a more Apostolic manner so that they are using the gifts of the Spirit and the King's authority to take back what the enemy had stolen. They will therefore be able to extend God's Kingdom here on Earth.

At KINGDOM CONNECTIONS, we endeavor to encourage, motivate, and equip individuals to walk in greater maturity, wisdom, character, holiness and power. Inspired by Jesus' mentoring of His disciples, we will equip and prepare you by the process of Transformation and Empowerment to become a passionate builder of God's Kingdom by helping you to acquire knowledge of and then embrace a Biblical Kingdom Worldview and a Kingdom mindset.

It is our desire for you to receive a vision of God's Grand Plan and as a result dedicate yourself to walk the narrow way and in the process find empowerment to release God's power for effective ministry to people in need. In order to do so, you will be exhorted to accept the challenges faced by every Christian as they learn what it means to be a 21st Century Overcomer for Jesus Christ. As you involve yourself in the process of Transformation and Empowerment, you are participating in Kingdom Living.

MAKING HIM KNOWN

We marvel at the signs and wonders done through certain Evangelists and Preachers. We see God showing His power and love by healing the sick and doing miracles in the midst of the people. We give honor to those whom honor is due because we know that God places certain men and women into positions who are using their gifts to further the advancement of the Kingdom of God.

We are excited to talk about their faith, their gifts, their (this or that) as if they are the only ones that God uses. We long for the day it will happen in our church or even through our own ministry.

Well my friend, it can happen right where you are. You do not have to wait for the "gifted one" to come to town. You can be the "gifted one". You were *BORN TO RULE*.

However, before we run to pick up Moses' rod or Elijah's mantle, let's be reminded of the song I first heard when I was about 10 years old, "If you can't wear the cross you can't wear the crown".

Ministry comes in many different forms, but whatever form it takes; it is service. In the OT it was the Kings, the Priests, the Prophets; these were the servants of God. They exercised mediation between God and Man. In the NT, Christ himself became the mediator between God and men, the unique priest who offered up the sacrifice for salvation.

Our function as servants has changed but the same heart of the servant is needed to carry out the work that Jesus, the Christ had started. If we are to perform that same quality of service, the same sacrifice of self and submission to the king is required. The Master said it best when He gave the Apostle John the promise of entering into the Father's glory,

"The hour has come that the Son of Man should be glorified. Most assuredly, I say to you, unless a grain of wheat falls into the ground and dies, it remains alone; but if it dies, it produces much grain. He who loves his life will lose it, and he who hates his life in this world will keep it

17

for eternal life. If anyone serves Me, let him follow Me; and where I am, there My servant will be also. If anyone serves Me, him My Father will honor." John 12:23-26

Jesus is Lord of His church but He too came to serve and not be served. We are not greater than our master is, therefore, He has given His church spiritual gifts that we can use to serve our brethren and also to proclaim Him and make Him known to the world.

There are various gifts but the same Spirit and therefore ALL of us that call Christ our King can exercise ministry to those in need. It is not for the precious few but for the many. We ALL have a place in Christ's Church to find a place of service. It matters not your age, race, education, gender, your intelligence or your social-economic status; God has called us ALL to serve – to minister.

The truths that you will encounter in the pages that follow will prepare you to take your rightful place in the hall of fame that God is creating. All that God requires of you is your OBEDIENCE AND FAITHFULNESS.

As you go on passed: the Knowing your Mission, the Need for Brokenness, the Call of God, and Receiving a Vision, you will enter a doorway that will lead to a life that will rattle the very gates of Hell.

Your faith will increase as you sense the presence of God with you. Your compassion will thrust you into the arena of the helpless and hopeless. You will pray with great effectiveness and you will confront the forces of darkness and be victorious. Sounds exciting, doesn't it? Well, it is.

Because of what has happened to you, you will leave the confines of the church building and will go out into the highways and byways in search of fulfillment. Jesus said to His disciples, *"I have meat that you know not of"*. Jesus found fulfillment as He ministered in the power of the Holy Spirit. You will find the same fulfillment as you do the same.

18

As you move from one chapter to another, you will grow in your faith and understanding of how the Holy Spirit operates in the supernatural. From your participating in the Kingdom Principles in BORN TO RULE, you have already learned how to be led by the Spirit as you moved along the narrow way to maturity. You have already learned to cooperate with the Holy Spirit in order that He could transform you.

You learned that we needed to have a Kingdom Worldview. Most likely, there were some adjustments made along the way as you allowed the Holy Spirit to make that transformation. There will be additional adjustments necessary now as you learn to become a Kingdom Builder.

What we normally consider miraculous has to do with either bodily healing or spiritual deliverance. These two areas of ministry have evoked thoughts of "faith Healing" or exorcism. Because of their bad reputation, both are dismissed as emotional or fake. Let us not, however throw the child out with the bath water. The Bible has a lot to say about both of these means of bringing wholeness to God's people.

There are a few things that you must understand and accept if you are going to, "work the works of God". In BORN TO RULE, you found, it is the Holy Spirit that transforms. You will now experience the Holy Spirit as He empowers you. You have learned to be sensitive to the leading and quickening of the Holy Spirit, now you must learn to let the Holy Spirit reveal what the Father wants to do, and then be obedient to those revelations, images, visions or dreams.

A KINGDOM WHICH CANNOT BE SHAKEN

Six things to keep in mind as you read this book:

- Our walk with God is all about Relationship and Fellowship

- All truths are parallel (spiritual truth is found in the physical realm revealing the truths of the spiritual)

- It is the Holy Spirit that Transforms (Maturity) and Empowers (Kingdom Building)

- God really does make His way easy to understand.

- A SHOEBOX APPROACH - I HAVE BEEN TEACHING THIS COURSE FOR MANY YEARS. THERE ARE SOME SECTIONS THAT MY STUDENTS HAVE FOUND MORE DIFFICULT TO UNDERSTAND OR ACCEPT. THESE SECTIONS ARE FORMATTED WITH SMALL CAPS. DO NOT AUTOMATICALLY DISCARD THE INFORMATION IF YOU FIND IT DIFFICULT TO PROCESS. I ENCOURAGE YOU TO SET ASIDE THIS INFORMATION. IT MAY HELP TO PUT IT IN A SHOEBOX ON A SHELF TO BE CONSIDERED LATER. This is OK; I've been doing it for years.

- Some things are very important for your understanding. When you see this shaded background, stop and reread the material to make sure you fully comprehend its meaning. If not then put it in your shoebox.

Chapter 1
Hearing The Voice of God

"Rhema" is a Greek word that denotes that which is spoken, what is uttered in speech or writing. "Logos", on the other hand denotes a statement made by someone or what is written. The written Bible is the Logos of God, while the Rhema of God is when God speaks directly to you or reveals something to you personally.

Without an understanding and without having an experience of "Rhema" what you do may be Biblical, good, and profitable but it will not be as a direct revelation from God. Therefore, it is important that you take time to build your relationship with the Holy Spirit. I hope that you have already begun to do this as you spent time reading our last book, *BORN TO RULE*.

WHEN IT BECOME PERSONAL

Rhema is hearing a voice and knowing it is **His voice**, not someone else's voice. Rhema is not your words but His word, spoken with His mouth directly into your spirit that goes forth to produce His Will; the results that He desires. Rhema is communication from God to our heart.

Western Christians are experiencing two problems!

First problem - Rules vs. Love. The majority of those who go by the name "Christian" live by a set of rules, a code of ethics, a list of laws to follow. Living in such a way might be religious but it is not Christianity. Christianity is a Spiritual Experience between a loving God and His Disciples. In various situations we try to "figure out", WWJD, instead of allowing the Spirit to reveal his Will and then transform us into his image.

From our first book, we found out that we not only could know ABOUT God, we can experience Him. We do not just say a Sinners Prayer, we bear witness to the fact that the Holy Spirit has convicted us of our sin and that we are a child of God. We can testify of a peace that surpasses all the understanding of the world's wisest men and that we KNOW-that we KNOW that our sins are forgiven. We have found the Bible, not to be simply words on a page to be studied and memorized but words that have come alive as the Holy Spirit "quickens" our heart as He brings revelation.

You might have started reading the Bible looking for a list of steps, keys, and techniques for a better life, but you found out that you needed to move beyond that to engage in a pursuit of Jesus Christ. A Spiritual Experience makes real the Love that God has for us and makes real the Love that we have for Him. Therefore, Christianity is more than religious rules to live by; it is a love relationship with the King of Kings. It is an encounter with the Father and the Son through the indwelling work of the Holy Spirit. Love like this is created through communication.

When God brought the Israelites out of Egypt, He wanted to speak to them directly but they chose instead to be governed by a set of laws. The Israelites returned to their tents, leaving Moses to speak with God and then relay the message.

The Church today is very much like the Old Testament Israelites. Once the laws are learned, there is a certainty as to what one is supposed to do. There is no extra effort exerted, as it might be when we are involved in a relationship. Building a relationship takes time, effort, sacrifice, giving, understanding and adding value to the other person's life.

2nd Problem – Rationalism vs. Revelation - We are concerned with our spirit and how the Mind is involved in developing a relationship with God. In the thirteenth century, Thomas Aquinas, however, was doing just the opposite; he put down the basis for exalting the Mind (Rationalism). Since then, the Western

Hemisphere has embraced an overemphasis on reason. In fact, in the 18th century, this age was often called, "the age of reason".

From Wikipedia, the free encyclopedia:

The Age of Reason: Being an Investigation of True and Fabulous Theology, a deistic treatise written by eighteenth-century British radical and American revolutionary Thomas Paine, critiques institutionalized religion and challenges the inerrancy of the Bible. Paine advocates reason in the place of revelation; leading him to reject miracles and to view the Bible as an ordinary piece of literature rather than as a divinely inspired text.

We asked the following question in BORN TO RULE, "since we are in a personal conflict with evil, what part does the MIND play in winning or losing the battle?" We stated, "The mind is the control center for all our dreams, hopes, fears and faith. It is here that we make decisions and vocalize what is in our heart. The mind is the center of our consciousness that generates thoughts, feelings, ideas, and stores knowledge and memories."

The Bible can be studied rationally. We can uses our mind and learn many facts about God. We can learn; God is All Powerful, He loves us, and that He has come to save us from our sins and much more. However, unless the Holy Spirit makes the Word come alive, it is of no use. It is as if we hear but do not understand, see but do not comprehend. Jesus spoke in Parables to the people because He wanted people to follow Him, not because they understand what He was saying with their mind but because they heard Him speak to their spirit.

Through rationalism, Christians in the West have relied less and less on Spirit to spirit encounters. We have increasingly used the left hemisphere of our mind (the part that works with logic and analysis) while relying less and less on the right side of our mind that focuses on pictures, intuition and emotions. Our desire, as 21st Century Disciples is to use the right side without throwing out the left side.

Understanding Truth

Do we understand truth with our mind or with our spirit? I Cor. 2:9-10 tells us, *"Eye has not seen, nor ear heard, Nor have entered into the heart of man the things which God has prepared for those who love Him." But God has revealed them to us through His Spirit. For the Spirit searches all things, yes, the deep things of God"* NKJV

Therefore, we come to know truth through our heart or spirit, rather than because of our mind. God reveals truth about Himself and life in general through our spirit, which our natural senses can never comprehend. We thank God for all that we are. We know that each part of our being (body, soul and spirit) has a part to play in bringing about God's Grand Plan that He has for us. However, God has made our spirit to function in such a way that we can hear His voice and have direct communication with Him.

What we are saying is this: with God, we can have inner subjective experiences in our mind (the right side). Through insight, we receive revelation from him, and He illuminates Scripture to us. Through intuition, we sense the promptings of the Holy Spirit and the voice of God. Our life in the spirit is then an intuitive, spiritual, inner, heart experience.

Christianity has as its base, Truth. Jesus said, *I am the Way, the Truth, and the life. You shall know the Truth and the Truth shall make you free. Thy Word is Truth.* The Holy Spirit is the Spirit of Truth. The Bible says that God cannot lie. The Word of God says that God has sent the Holy Spirit into our hearts, saying "Abba Father" thereby opening the door of opportunity for us to have direct, ongoing, personal experience with the Living God.

The Apostle Paul says in Rom 8:14-17, "For *as many **as are led** by the Spirit of God, these are sons of God. For you did not receive the spirit of bondage again to fear, but you received the Spirit of adoption by whom we cry out, "Abba, Father". The Spirit Himself bears witness with our spirit that we are children of God, and if children, then heirs — heirs of God and joint heirs with Christ, if indeed we suffer with Him, that we may also be glorified together".*

24

He goes on to say in Gal 5:16-18, *"I say then: Walk in the Spirit, and you shall not fulfill the lust of the flesh. For the flesh lusts against the Spirit, and the Spirit against the flesh; and these are contrary to one another, so that you do not do the things that you wish. But if you are **led by the Spirit**, you are not under the law".*

If we allow ourselves to be restricted to using our mind only, we will lose the opportunity to relate to our Father and His Son, our King in such a way that produces an intimate love relationship. We too will lose the opportunity to minister to those in need using the nine Gifts of the Spirit. We will forfeit receiving guidance through dreams and visions and have a fruitful and effective prayer life and lose out on having an awesome time of worship whether in private or in a corporate setting.

Faith and Rhema – "See that you do not refuse Him who speaks"

Faith is what releases the Power. The Bible tells us that faith comes by hearing and hearing by the Word of God. The Word of God is the Will of God. When we **hear** and are obedient to the word (submissive with joy), we come into a deeper fellowship with the King. It is from this fellowship that God speaks and faith makes its appearance.

When we speak out in faith that which we hear, a power is released to do whatever God wants His Word to do. That which we hear is a Rhema Word. Rhema is Spirit to spirit communication – where the Holy Spirit speaks directly to your spirit.

The Apostle Paul confronted the Galatians because they were forsaking their relationship with the Holy Spirit and returning again to the law. Listen to what he says in Gal 3:1-9

O foolish Galatians! Who has bewitched you that you should not obey the truth, before whose eyes Jesus Christ was clearly portrayed among you as crucified? This only I want to learn from you: Did you receive the Spirit by the works of the law, or by the hearing of faith? Are you so foolish? Having begun in the Spirit, are you now being made perfect by the flesh? Have you suffered so many things in vain — if indeed it was in vain?

25

Therefore He who supplies the Spirit to you and works miracles among you, does He do it by the works of the law, or by the hearing of faith? — just as Abraham "believed God, and it was accounted to him for righteousness." Therefore know that only those who are of faith are sons of Abraham. And the Scripture, foreseeing that God would justify the Gentiles by faith, preached the gospel to Abraham beforehand, saying, "In you all the nations shall be blessed." So then those who are of faith are blessed with believing Abraham.

Again, it is said in Heb 12:25-29

"See that you do not refuse Him who speaks. For if they did not escape who refused Him who spoke on earth, much more shall we not escape if we turn away from Him who speaks from heaven, whose voice then shook the earth; but now He has promised, saying, "Yet once more I shake not only the earth, but also heaven." Now this, "Yet once more," indicates the removal of those things that are being shaken, as of things that are made, that the things which cannot be shaken may remain.

*Therefore, since we are receiving **a kingdom which cannot be shaken**, let us have grace, by which we may serve God acceptably with reverence and godly fear. For our God is a consuming fire".*

We, as Overcomers, must always be sensitive to the promptings of the Holy Spirit. Jesus speaks and the Holy Spirit is charged to bring His voice to us. The Holy Spirit is like the gentle dove, so sensitive and sweet. He will not force Himself on any of us. By our sin, we can grieve Him; by our pride, we can quench His coming, and send him away. Satan is constantly at work to dull our spiritual senses and turn our attention away from hearing with our spirit <u>toward</u> understanding with our mind.

The coming of the Holy Sprit is not just an objective, or a spiritual event that was foretold at a specific time in history. His coming is an inward happening. It is something that happens to every "Born Again" believer. His coming is not only for the mature Christian, He is here for all that are starting their walk with Christ. He floods our very being so that out of us can flow rivers of living water.

We said at the beginning of Book One in, *BORN TO RULE*, "All truth must come through revelation. Therefore, we must be sensitive to the Holy Spirit and His promptings, His guidance, and His leading. He is easily grieved by sin and will not force Himself on you. You must develop this relationship."

The Holy Spirit is the Spirit of Revelation and what He is bringing to the Church is, SPIRIUAL VISION. He first opens our eyes to see the Kingdom and He fills in the "rest of the story" as we live out our life in Christ.

The Nation of Israel lost its ability to SEE because of they had forsaken their God and had gone after other gods.

LISTEN FOR THE VOICE

There are no other questions that trouble Christians today than, "How do I hear the voice of God" and "How do I know that it is God's voice and not just my own thoughts"? We hear a lot of Christians say, "God said" and we wonder, whose voice did they really hear?

Jesus said, *"My sheep hear My voice, and I know them, and they follow Me."* You don't get to recognize someone's voice and know their heart without spending time with them. It is over time that we sense their presence, even when we don't hear them. We even know what they are going to say before they even say it.

Our goal is to develop our spirit. It is out of our spirit that we live for Christ. Our spirit will direct us through unprompted, unstructured, and spur of the moment thought, idea, word, feeling or vision, which are brought to it, by our communion with the Holy Spirit.

OUR READING AND STUDYING OF THE BIBLE DOES NOT DEVELOP OUR SPIRIT; OUR SPIRIT IS DEVELOPED BY USING IT IN COMMUNION WITH GOD. THE HOLY SPIRIT HELPS OUR UNDERSTANDING AS WE MEDITATE ON THE WORD BUT DIRECTION IS RECEIVED BY "WAITING" QUIETLY UPON THE LORD ALLOWING HIM TO INJECT HIS THOUGHTS INTO OUR HEART.

You can be a great teacher of History, Math or Science by developing your mind but you cannot be led or flow in the gifts of the Spirit unless you know the Word (logos) and are sensitive to the voice of God within (Rhema).

27

As I am writing this my virus protection keeps popping up telling me my computer is not fully protected. It is bothersome but beneficial; the point is this, our knowledge of God's Word (stored in our mind) is like the virus protection, it checks each revelation we receive in our spirit making sure that it is in line with the Word. If it is not then we need to discard it.

Divine Encounter

In, BORN TO RULE, we mentioned the disciple having a Divine Encounter. It is like two cars coming towards two crossing roads and meeting at the intersection precisely at the same moment. It is a chance encounter. God's sovereignty deals with timing, so He is the one that determines the WHEN of the encounter.

There are times when further "encounters" are determined by our obedience. In I Kings 17 there is a story of Elijah. On several occasions, God has an encounter with Elijah and tells him to go a certain place and He would meet him "there". It was at the "there" that the blessing would be found and be available. Just like the two cars meeting at the intersection, meeting God takes place at a certain place. Note; the "place" is also in God's sovereignty.

Encounters occur while in the presence of God. Each encounter is personal; it does not come second hand. It is during these personal encounters that you are learning to TRUST God and He is revealing to you whether or not He can TRUST You.

What can we expect when we have such an encounter? Here are six things to look for.

1. They are much like our own thoughts except we will sense that they are coming from the heart and not from the brain. Why is this so; because they are spontaneous and not premeditated?

2. They will be spoken in the first person, right from God to you.

3. They will cause a response from within you such as a sense of excitement, conviction, faith, life, awe, or peace.

4. When accepted as from God, there comes with them strength and an enthusiasm to carry out the will of God.

5. As we develop our spirit, the sense of knowing that the "encounter" was from God, the sharper and clearer will become the voice of God.

6. Since God's ways are not our ways, these spontaneous thoughts, most likely, will be outside our comfort zone.

In the process of developing our spirit and distinguishing the Voice of God, we are learning how to separate THE SPONTANEOUS thoughts that are originating from the Holy Spirit and those thoughts that are coming from our mind.

Here is how many others and I have described their experiences:

- An impression came to me

- In my mind, I saw a girl sitting at a table

- I jotted down the thoughts

- Sometimes God's voice came as an audible voice, "an inner audible voice"

- I received a vision

- I had a deep impression

- It came to me as words imprinted quietly on my spirit

Here is how I first learn to develop my spirit to hear Spirit to spirit messages.

My Pastor, Dr. C.E. Fast, told me to sit down with the children in front of the TV or while they were playing and begin to read my Bible. I was not to be involved with the TV or the children but to be still and read. Read, yes but as I read, listen for the Holy Spirit speaking to me regarding what I was reading. Does this make sense?

As I did this, my life began to be transformed. I began to see things, not from my perspective, but from God's. It was if I was taken into his confidence in order that I might have the mind of Christ.

Here are some examples from my own life with various ways the Holy Spirit has led me. Some of the following are chance encounters (God initiated) or are answers to prayer and God is leading.

- I was at a Morris Curello crusade in downtown Chicago. On offering night, **I was impressed** to give $100.00. You might think, No big deal. Well, it was a big deal, Bea and I only had $110.00 to our name. I went home and told Bea and she said; WHAT? The next day, however, she came and said, "I too think it's from God". The giving of that $100.00 released us from being a **Taker** to being a **Giver**. It provided us with the knowledge that we can TRUST God and by our obedience, we said to God, you can trust us.

- A few months after the above incident, **I had a dream/vision** of us having foster children and the home that we would live in. I went to Dr. Fast and told him what happened. He said, "I too believe it is of God, just proceed slowly and DON"T give up if things don't happen right away or some disappointments happen along the way." Oh, how wonderful is Godly counsel.

I contacted a Realtor who took me to three houses. When we came to the third house, I knew it was the same as I had seen in the vision. We went back to her office and she asked me if I was going to put in an offer. I said NO. She was quite confused considering all that I had told her. She asked why. I told her that God had only **told** me to find the house, not buy it. Four months later, as I was coming home on the train, God spoke to me again and **told** me to go and buy that house.

When I got to the Realtor, I told her what I came to do, but she was very indignant and said, "How do you know it is still for sale?" I told her, "Because God told me to buy it". It was still for sale! We sat down and figured what I could afford and the amount was $4,000 less than the offer they had already turned down. I said that is not my problem so send them the offer anyway. Because they had just become Christian, in their new home in another state, they **felt that they should accept the offer.**

After two months, the bank finally got back to me and called me on a Saturday morning. This is what they said, "Mr. Farrier, we can not give you a 90% mortgage but we can give you an 80% mortgage. Here was the problem; I had to borrow the down payment from my parents because I only had $10.00, remember.

I did not have the first 10% and now they want another 10%, plus the closing costs. What would you do? If I backed out, I would get back the earnest money. If I could not come up with the rest of the down payment, I would lose the $2,000 that my parents loaned me.

I offered a quick prayer to the God who had given me the Vision. It was for real or it was not. God gave assurance; I knew that I knew that God had spoken to me. I told them, "Go for it"!

We moved into that house with two beautiful foster children, almost one year after I had received the Vision. We came up with the money and had $3.00 + left when we left the lawyers office. Oh, the goodness of God.

- God used this same way of speaking to me regarding three other houses that we moved into over the years, however not so dramatically.

- When I first went to college in Ohio, God woke me upon in the wee hours of the morning. **I was directed** to read John 12: 25-26. He then **told me** (An inner audible voice) not to look for a job but the job will come to me. That went against everything that I had read in the Bible. I obeyed for a month and then I went and found a job. The day I was to start, I knew that I knew that I was being disobedient. I went over to the store where I was to start and quit. That night, I received a knock on the door at 11:00 PM and was told about a job opening. I, however, needed to go through the state employment office. I went down there the next day and applied. There was one catch to the job; the applicant needed to be unemployed for at least 30 days. Because of God's leading, I qualified.

- While attending Bible College in Ohio, I was looking at a magazine that advertised another college that was located in Florida. Again, **I was impressed** to look into it. I received the info and sent in my application. One day I was reading my Bible and this time I **heard an inner voice** saying you are accepted, sell your house and go. I sold my house almost immediately, packed a truck and left. How did God honor my trust in him? He gave me a vision of a house in Lakeland, FL, near Southeastern University (I received my acceptance from SU two weeks after we arrived), the owner of our new house sold the house way under market value, my new neighbor had a friend who knew about a job opening and offered it to me and much much more.

- I was reading in John where Jesus said that He only does what the Father is doing. I asked God, since I was asked to preach in New Hampshire that evening, what He was doing. **He showed me** a man in the back of the church that had a severe leg injury and was in tremendous pain. While I was preaching I was looking for this man but didn't see him. During the ministry time, I walked to the back of the church and there he was. I reached out and laid my hand on him. I spoke to his leg to be healed in the name of Jesus and then grasped his hand and pulled him to his feet. He had been in this condition for several years and had been a part of this church for most of his life.

- My mother and I went to church on a Wednesday night, thinking that the service started at 7:30. We got there around 7:40 but the service began at 7:00. After only a few minutes, someone gave a message in tongues. **A heart racing feeling came over me and thoughts appeared in my mind instantly.** I knew that the Holy Spirit had given to me the interpretation. I gave it and after the service people were astonished because what I had spoken gave meaning to all that had transpired before my mother and I arrived.

- As being part of the prayer team, I minister to people when they come forward after the service. A woman came forward, but without her telling me her need the **Holy Spirit put pictures in my mind** and I just prayed in according to what I saw. When I saw her a little while later, she was so excited because I had prayed directly to her need. I invited her to our Kingdom Builders class. She came and one night, one of the other students mentioned that she was plagued with migraine headaches. Normally I would pray immediately **but something inside said,** "Tell her you will pray for her next week". Next week, the woman that came because of prayer in church, was there but because of circumstances, brought her son and daughter also. After the class, we gathered together to pray for the woman that had migraines and found out that the daughter of the other woman (she is a medical Doctor) also suffered from migraines, maybe even more so. We took authority over these migraines, cast them out and they have been free ever since; to God be the Glory.

- I was driving my mother-in-law from Chicago to Toledo in order for her to catch a bus back to Rochester, N.Y. I had no idea where the bus terminal was located, so as we were approaching the city on the expressway, I asked the Lord to direct me. As we got closer to the city **the Holy Spirit impressed me** to get off at the next exit. When I got off I was **again impressed** to turn left. We went about two or three blocks, I **was impressed** to turn right; there it was.

When ministering overseas in third world countries, all you can rely on is the faithfulness of the Holy Spirit. When you are far out in the small villages, the only protection you have is God. The Gifts of the Holy Spirit are the only thing that will convince the people of the reality of the living God.

Some of the examples are involving one or more of the Gifts of the Spirit (I Cor. 12) but the others are Spirit to spirit communication. I can continue for some time with more examples, but NOW it is your turn. If you have not experienced Spirit to spirit encounters, NOW is the time to prepare yourself to do so. You may have experienced them but did not recognize it and never acted upon them.

Get out a notebook especially for the use of writing them down. As you do so, Faith will increase and continue to increase, as you are obedient to this promptings.

Note: The above are some of my experiences with great outcomes. Conversely, I can tell you hundreds of others where I have missed it. It could have been because of sin in my life, or when I was preoccupied, or just didn't want to listen. We all go through seasons in life that we are not proud. Check these people out in the Old Testament; David, Sampson, Saul, all these men had the anointing then lost it foolishly. Only David and Sampson, however, humbled themselves and had it return. It did nevertheless; cost Sampson his life and David his son. In the New Testament, Barnabas restored the writer of the Gospel of Mark, who had left the work with Paul on his first missionary journey.

When Jesus ascended into heaven, He told his disciples that the Holy Spirit would lead them and guide them into all truth. He told them that He would not leave them comfortless. The Holy Spirit, being the Spirit of the Lord, is now taking the place of Jesus here on earth. We are to follow Him just as the early disciples had followed Jesus. He is just as much God as Jesus is God. He is the Spirit of the Lord.

Jesus is the King and as such, He has showed us how to bring people into the Kingdom. We are to lead people to the Kingdom where they first find the King as the door. They find the King, not dressed in kingly garments but the plain cloths of a carpenter. He holds out his nail scared hands as He welcomes them and bids them enter. His voice is not that of a king that has the sound of thunder and piercing like that of lightning but like that of a gentle shepherd.

As they respond to his love, they are humbled, bow down and soon find themselves repenting of their sins. When they feel a hand on their shoulder, they will look up and when they do - they will look into the face of our Heavenly Father. They will hear of the voice of God saying the words they have been longing to hear, "You are forgiven". This hearing, "you are forgiven" is the Believers first "Rhema" experience.

Chapter 2
Understanding Ministry

As we go from becoming an "Overcomer" to doing the works of an "Overcomer", we progress down the pathway that leads to "Maturity". The vision is ever before us, and we desire to earn the right to Reign with The King of kings and the Lord of lords. Therefore, we must captured HIS PURPOSE in our heart and be ready to move on.

In order to make Christ known in such a way that His life, death, resurrection and ascension has an impact upon people's lives that last for an eternity, we must go through a preparation process. In this process, we acquire the foundation upon which to build the ministry Christ is giving to us and extend His Kingdom. This chapter and the next will cause us to concentrate on the preparation for ministry. All the mighty men and women of God have needed preparation in these following four areas:

- Knowing Your Kingdom Mission

- The Need for Brokenness

- The Call of God

- Receiving a Vision

KNOWING THE KINGDOM MISSION

Definition of mission: A task assigned, an act of ending, a specific task to which a person or group is charged.

- A mission is always specific, has an end in mind and is something that needs to be accomplished.

- A mission always involves people; people must sense the importance of the mission, the possibility of accomplishment, and the consequences of a failed mission.

- A mission is given; it is the desire, the passion of the one giving the mission to others. The passion for the mission must be caught as well as the understanding of the mission.

Some would understand The Mission as the Great Commission found in Matt. 28:16-20; Mark 16:14-18; Luke 24:36-49; John 20: 19-23; Acts 1: 6-8, yet they are falling far short of what is called for by our Father.

Our Lord's mission is often taken piece meal: meaning one group emphasizes certain aspects of the Great Commission and another emphasizes other aspects. Because of this, we have seen the emergence of the Soul Saving ministries, the Healing ministries, the Deliverance ministries, the Servant hood ministries and the Social Gospel ministries.

If you are going to completely understanding your mission or assignment, you must embrace the full purpose of God.

Let us revisit Chapters three & four from the first book, *BORN TO RULE* and see again; The Kingdom Established, Lost, Reclaimed and Re-established.

Why the Kingdom was established?

God's great desire was that those who were created in their image and likeness, would have dominion over the Earth. This would allow Him to extend His spiritual kingdom to the physical realm. The same government, however, would rule Earth as well as Heaven. The kingdom, including its Government and culture would be patterned after the Kingdom of Heaven where He dwells.

What led to the Kingdom to be lost?

Satan, having been thrown out from the presence of God, sees his opportunity to avenge himself and suffer God a big blow which he hopes will lead to him having his own kingdom and receiving the worship that he so covets. Just as he had deceived 1/3 of the angels of heaven, he deceives man into thinking that he too could be like God. Man falls for the deception but soon realizes that he is doomed with the same fate as the deceiver. He is expelled from the presence of God and is kicked out of the Garden of Eden.

Satan now rules the Earth system of government and wrecks havoc on the human race. He does not want to lose his kingdom so he continues his attempt to thwart God's plan while at the same time unwittingly playing into God's hand.

How was the Kingdom reclaimed?

Jesus, the Father's Word, came to this earth and took the form of a man that He might be the propitiation for our sins. Jesus, by His life, death, burial, resurrection and ascension destroys the power that Sin and deception has over people. Jesus destroyed the work of His enemy and in the process, set people free. He made it possible for man, by repentance, to have their sins forgiven and be reconciled to the Father.

How will the Kingdom be re-established?

God the Father sent His Spirit into the hearts of Man and by doing so, brought conviction of sin, righteousness and judgment. Man could either respond to this LOVE and MERCY of God or turn his back on the offer. Man now has the option to enter into a covenant relationship with God with terms lasting for an eternity. Jesus made it possible for us to be reconciled and therefore, be restored to citizenship and eligible for ambassadorship that we might work the works of God and extend His Kingdom.

With a "new" spirit we are now being transformed into the image and likeness of Christ and having the power of the Holy Spirit we are now able to take back what the Devil has stolen.

Our Mission:

Part One – Restore man to Fellowship with his Creator

In order to restore man to a place of fellowship, we must wage war against Satan and capture the hearts of men. It sounds simple but it is not. If it were, the world would already be won for Jesus. The Church has lost its first love, has intermingled with false religions, and has accepted the behavior and attitudes of the world. The Church has activity but it has forgotten its purpose, and has no heart for the loss or desire to live totally for God. Therefore, before the Church can begin the work given to it by King Jesus, it must be awakened to hear the voice of the Spirit.

Sinners are separated from the love of God; therefore, the process of restoration begins by showing that God loves them. We need to tell them of His love but even more so, to show them the love of God that is within us. People need to know that we accept them as they are and so does God, their Creator.

It is love that breaks down the barriers of resistance and doubt. It is love that opens the ears of the skeptic and the heart of the fearful. Love says to them that they are valued as a person. Love reveals our willingness to sacrifice time, energy, and sometimes money. When we show people this kind of love, they are more open to the love of God that confronts their sinfulness and His solution to its consequences.

Paul said, *"I'm not ashamed of the Gospel of Christ for it is the power of God unto salvation"*. Paul had an encounter with God that changed his life. This wonderful change from sinner to saint forever captured his heart and he turned from prosecuting the Christians to being one of them.

Paul was willing to do whatever it took to win some for Christ. He put himself on the firing line time after time. He was willing to spend and be spent for Christ sake. He knew who he was and the mission he was given, first as a disciple and then as an Apostle.

We use to sing this song, years ago, "Be Bold, Be Strong for the Lord thy God is with thee." Just the singing of this verse raised our hopes for victory. Boldness rose up within us and moved us forward into battle. It is what Paul had and it is what Satan is afraid of - our BOLDNESS.

Luke writes, "Now when they saw the BOLDNESS of Peter and John, and perceived that they were uneducated, common men, they wondered; and they recognized that they had been with Jesus". They warned them not to speak anymore in this name (Jesus).

When Peter and John returned to their friends, they gathered together and prayed. What did they pray for? They prayed for BOLDNESS to speak the Word and believed that God would stretch out His hand to heal and perform signs and wonders through the name of His holy servant, Jesus. As a result, the place in which they were gathered together was shaken; and they were all filled with the Holy Spirit and they all spoke the word of God with BOLDNESS.

To tell your loved one, your friends, and your co-workers that they need to repent (change their mind) is not easy. If we are going to do this, we must have the same mindset as Paul. Paul's mindset was to introduce to the Churches a Kingdom Culture. It was the culture of the Kingdom that unbelievers saw that opened the door for the sharing of the Gospel. But, it was Boldness that caused them to proclaim, "Repent for the Kingdom is at hand".

Part Two – Make Disciples

There is a lovely hymn that says, "I'll go where you want me to go dear Lord, I'll do what you want me to do. I'll say what you want me to say dear Lord, I'll be what you want me to be". This almost sums it all up concisely. Disciples see the same needs as their Lord and commit themselves in complete obedience, to work with the Holy Spirit in meeting that need.

We would be wrong in suggesting that one can be or that we can make Overcomers just by having them attend a Overcomers class or by reading a book (no matter how enlightening). This book when read and if presented in a class environment will hopefully give others a new mindset and expand their vision and their faith. The making of an Overcomer, however, is a process and is really only accomplished in the context of love, encouragement, and correction. It was in this small group context that Jesus not only taught but also showed through example a Kingdom lifestyle and demonstrated the power of the Holy Spirit.

The cost of becoming an Overcomer is great. The world may see this way of life as living in uncertainty. Nevertheless, to the Overcomer, it is a life of continuous certainty in things not seen.

The Father's great desire is for His children to reign with His Son Jesus. In order to do so, His children must live this new life that has been given them. Others must see the life of Jesus in our words, feelings, actions and in our thoughts. This means that the outcome of our daily life must be the same as that of Jesus. Others must see Jesus in us and be touched by His love and power through us and smell the fragrance of life.

Peter says it so plainly in 2 Peter 1:2-12 regarding what we have been given in order to succeed:

"Grace and peace be multiplied to you in the knowledge of God and of Jesus our Lord; as His divine power has given to us all things that pertain to life and godliness, through the knowledge of Him who called us by glory and virtue, by which have been given to us exceedingly great and precious promises, that through these you may be partakers of the divine nature, having escaped the corruption that is in the world through lust".

He goes on to explain how this growth in the Faith can occur when he says, *"But also for this very reason, giving all diligence, add to your faith virtue, to virtue knowledge, to knowledge self-control, to self-control perseverance, to perseverance godliness, to godliness brotherly kindness, and to brotherly kindness love. For if these things are yours and abound, you will be neither barren nor unfruitful in the knowledge of our Lord Jesus Christ. For he who lacks these things is shortsighted, even to blindness, and has forgotten that he was cleansed from his old sins.*

It is one thing to be committed to the Lord and to follow Him personally in your life. It is quite another to pour your life into another and make disciples of them. This is what sets the true Disciple apart from the rest. He is interested in extending Christ's Kingdom. In other words, he is a Kingdom Builder. It is not enough to wage war against Satan and to share your faith with others, we must be about building a community of believers who show evidence of Christ's power, preparing ourselves for spiritual battle, and exhibiting, by our life style (our culture), our unreserved commitment to Christ and His Kingdom. It is only then that we will be World Changers.

The Church has become more of an organization and as such it has majored on the minors. It has spent its time teaching the Bible instead of centering its activity on building a relationship between the saints and their God. We build their mind, thinking; if people know about God that it will substitute for knowing God. The Church asks people to serve and serve they do, but unfortunately they receive the same condemnation as the Church at Ephesus; *"I know your works, your labor, your patience, and that you cannot bear those who are evil. And you have tested those who say they are apostles and are not, and have found them liars; and you have persevered and have patience, and have labored for My name's sake and have not become weary. Nevertheless, I have this against you, that you have left your first love"* Rev 2:2-4. Service without Love is just activity; it adds no lasting value to one being served.

Part Three – Restore man to a place of Dominion

Our Father has not set His Kingdom here on earth in order to have people to rule. He set His Kingdom here so those who He created could have a relationship with Him and they would rule or have dominion over that which He created.

A KINGDOM WHICH CANNOT BE SHAKEN

In Chapter Four of BORN TO RULE, we saw the importance of seeing every thing in the proper perspective; this included beginning at the proper starting point. Regarding man, Genesis 1:26-28 says it best, *"Then God said, "Let Us make man in Our image, according to Our likeness; let them have dominion over the fish of the sea, over the birds of the air, and over the cattle, over all the earth and over every creeping thing that creeps on the earth." So God created man in His own image; in the image of God He created him; male and female He created them. Then God blessed them, and God said to them, "Be fruitful and multiply; fill the earth and subdue it; have dominion over the fish of the sea, over the birds of the air, and over every living thing that moves on the earth."*

This is of upmost importance to God as this is the very purpose for creation. God put within man's spirit the desire to control his surroundings and extend Heaven's government to Earth. He is to use that which he has been given in a way that provides accomplishment, satisfaction and pleasure. It is in exercising dominion that man fulfills his purpose. Man's dominion is not to be implemented outside the boundaries of God's influence but as God's agent, representing the Kingdom of Heaven here on earth.

In order to for us to bring others into this place of dominion, we must first experience it ourselves. Just as you cannot bring someone into a place of redemption without knowing the Savior yourself, you cannot bring others to this place of dominion without firsthand experience. The Roman Centurion knew that to exercise authority he had to be under authority himself, therefore he says to Jesus, *"For I also am a man under authority, having soldiers under me. And I say to this one, 'Go,' and he goes; and to another, 'Come,' and he comes; and to my servant, 'Do this,' and he does it." Matt 8:9*

We are given a mandate to make the Name of our Lord known throughout the world. We must do more than tell others about Jesus, we must let them know that He is alive by demonstrating to others that we are indeed his Ambassadors and His power is real over all the earth.

44

Jesus brought to us a consciousness of the Kingdom of God, restored to us the true meaning of Holiness and Righteousness, and introduced us to the Holy Spirit. Jesus introduces us to the main principle that governs all of God's actions – The Cross. Jesus said, *"But he who is greatest among you shall be your servant. And whoever exalts himself will be humbled, and he who humbles himself will be exalted"*. He did all this so that Man would know how to rule, to have dominion.

We are to have Dominion – yes – but not at the expense of others. Jesus was the perfect example of one who exercised dominion. He came to minister to others, not to be ministered to.

Jesus demonstrated dominion in many ways. He demonstrated dominion when He healed the sick, turned water into wine, fed the 5,000 with two loaves and five fishes, calmed the storm, walked on water, and raised the dead. Whenever He preached about the Kingdom, people responded to the truth and followed Him. Everywhere He went He exercised dominion and turned the world right side up. He affected His surroundings and for this, the religious people wanted to kill Him.

THEREFORE, THE MISSION IS (1) RESTORE MAN TO FELLOWSHIP WITH HIS CREATOR (2) MAKE DISCIPLES (3) RESTORE MAN TO A PLACE OF DOMINION; THIS NO EASY TASK.

THE NEED FOR BROKENNESS

What can induce us to make God's Mission a priority in our lives? Before we can embark on the road to fulfill God's mission, we must experience, what we can call Brokenness. In "BORN TO RULE, we introduced the thought that because of Justification we have been given a new nature, however, we are still dealing with the flesh.

Our flesh is weak and prone to temptation; therefore, we must present our flesh to be crucified as Paul admonishes, *"And those who are Christ's have crucified the flesh with its passions and desires."* Gal 5:24-2

45

A KINGDOM WHICH CANNOT BE SHAKEN

In our moments of religious euphoria, we daydream of winning the world to Christ, healing the sick, setting the drug addict and alcoholic free, binding up the broken hearts that are suffering from divorce and separation. But our flesh cries out for attention and if not confronted, soon learns that if it cries loud enough and long enough it will get its own way and then becomes the one in control and our desire losses it passion. We do not want it to be this way; we do desire to do great things for God.

However, it is when we see our need for Brokenness that our dreams seem closer to fulfillment then before. Brokenness is God's work but we must present ourselves as a living sacrifice in order for the Holy Spirit to bring it about in our lives. Many of us struggle with a strong will, strong emotions and a strong mind therefore, it is imperative we recognize when it is God dealing with us and not attribute it to man. We must *know* that it is God and not just the consequences of our actions.

Brokenness cannot occur if our love of self is present. Within every man, a mechanism triggers self-preservation and if God is dealing with us, we put up barriers that block out the Holy Spirit so that He cannot work. Brokenness is, "going to the cross", "crucifying the flesh; is it any wonder that there is resistance to this work of the Holy Spirit.

Before we became new creatures in Christ, our spirit flowed through our soul picking up whatever the world deposited and then we expressed it in our body (through our actions and behavior). How much of the world affected our soul, depends on our culture, education, family background, religious training, or environment.

However, after we are "Born Again", the Holy Spirit comes to make God's Word alive in us as we read it, study, meditate on it. The Spirit and the Word working together now begins to wash us and cleanses us from the deposits left by the world.

Our fruitfulness or effectiveness is dependent on the Holy Spirit's power being able to be released through us to touch others. His release will only come about as a result of our Brokenness.

Jesus gives an illustration of the Brokenness principle. From John 12:20-22 we read of certain Greeks who had come to the feast in Jerusalem to worship and they came and asked of Philip – *"we would like to see Jesus"*. Why did they want to have an audience with Jesus? They had made the wrong assumption; they assumed that the miracles that Jesus performed came from the "man" Jesus. In truth, they came through the "man" Jesus and were the result of His brokenness. The power to do the miracles resided not in the "man" Jesus but the Holy Spirit who was in Jesus.

Jesus was at the height of his ministry – for 3 years He had gone throughout Israel preaching repentance and proclaiming that the Kingdom was at hand. Just a few days earlier, as He came into the city, they were throwing palm branches on the street in front of Him and crying, *"Hosanna: Blessed is the King of Israel that cometh in the name of the Lord."*

Jesus, however, never allowed Himself to be caught up in the praise of others for His mighty acts or for whom others thought Him to be. He never strutted nor flaunted His power. When they came to see Jesus, He stopped them in their tracks when He says, *"the hour is come, that the Son of man should be glorified. Verily, verily, I say unto you, expect a corn of wheat fall into the ground and die, it abides alone: but if it dies, it brings forth much fruit." He that loves his life shall lose it; and he that hates his life in this world shall keep it unto life eternal. If any man serves me, let him follow me; and where I am, there shall my servant be: if any man serve me, him will my father honor."*

In the story of Mary and the alabaster box, the Holy Spirit shows us another illustration of the principle of brokenness. It is only when the box is broken can the ointment be spilled out and the fragrance be a blessing to those around.

The point made in both of these accounts is this: the value is not in having a corn of wheat or in having a beautiful box filled with precious ointment. It is only when the corn of wheat dies can it bring forth life and only when the alabaster box is broken can a wonderful fragrance come from the ointment. The box is not more precious than the ointment and the grain is not more valuable than the life within.

Because Satan is forever protecting his kingdom, he goes all out to put a stop to the work of the dedicated worker for Christ. He is aware of the danger to his kingdom when God's people discover Brokenness; therefore, his priority is to keep us away from dealing with our flesh and kept busy with church work.

SATAN'S THREE PRIORITIES:

Satan's Priority # 1 – Keep us from having a Kingdom Worldview. Satan can handle us having a Biblical Man-centered Worldview because when we are concerned with our salvation, our healing, our problems, our church; he keeps us away from fulfilling God's purposes.

We often get side tracked from our original purpose by things that make happy the flesh for a little while but are far less satisfying then what was first proposed. Is not this the story of our life? Isn't this what has kept most of us from becoming what we had dreamed.

A father wants to take his son to a movie and McDonalds but finds that he is all dirty. He cleans him up but before they leave, the son gets side tracked by the new toys he received for his birthday. He forgets all about going with his dad; playing with his toys is more exciting to him than time spent with his father.

The Apostle John writes of the church at Ephesus; he knows their works, their toil, and their patience and endurance but he has this against them; they have abandoned their first love – they got side tracked.

The Christians of today are very much like those in the stories above. We partake of the grace of God only to become wholly distracted from the original purpose that He has for us. We become involved in what we perceive to be God's work instead of waiting to be led by the Holy Spirit.

All of the following men got side tracked: Noah, Abraham, Isaac, Jacob, and David. Read their stories and see how God had to deal with each one to bring them back to the purpose for which they were called. Read also of Joseph and note the difference.

Man is ever prone to interpret God's work as it benefits and relates to him. We are without concern for the realization of the yearning desire hidden in the heart of the Father. God has called us to a deeper and deeper fellowship and that means giving of ourselves to God, as God has given Himself to us. In Chapter four of BORN TO RULE, we have seen that man always wants to stop short of the deepest fellowship: the Fellowship of his Sufferings. Satan knows that continuous fellowship with the Son will lead to Brokenness and living wholly for God.

It is in this fellowship that the Holy Spirit does His work, like a Drill Sergeant responsible for developing a new recruit into a soldier. He puts us through the tough *courses* that we may become Holy and made ready to take our place to rule and reign with Christ. We may begin by loving Him for what He has done, but are soon transformed into loving Him for who He is.

Satan will do everything he can to get us to ignore God's discipline and revert to living from a Biblical Man-centered Worldview.

Satan's priority #2 - Keep us from sharing the Kingdom message and God's Grand Plan. Satan is not worried about individuals "getting saved" and living with a man-centered Worldview. He can keep them contained and even limit their effectiveness.

WHAT HE IS CONCERNED WITH IS; IF THEY GET A VISION OF GOD'S GRAND PLAN, DEDICATE THEIR LIVES TO WALK IN THE NARROW WAY AND UNITE UNDER ONE FLAG THEY WILL ACCOMPLISH GOD'S PURPOSE. IT IS THEN THAT HIS KINGDOM IS IN JEOPARDY. HE CANNOT LET THAT HAPPEN.

Satan has allowed the Church to tell people about Jesus' love, peace, healing power, and the promise of heaven without much of a fight. Why? Because he knows that God's people are reluctant to deal with the flesh and therefore will not pursue a Kingdom

Worldview, develop a Kingdom culture and seek to fulfill God's plan for Sonship.

Brokenness makes it possible for us to put aside the pleasures and benefits of this new life that God has given to us. This we are to do willingly in order to go and reconcile the unbeliever for whom Jesus also died.

Satan's priority #3 -To keep the Church from effectively fighting his kingdom, Satan has allowed us to have Bible studies, mission projects, and whatever else that keeps us from knowing of the brokenness needed for effective ministry.

Satan does not mind losing a battle here and there; he is concerned with losing his kingdom. Every effort Satan has put forth throughout the ages has had this in mind. The kingdom of this world can only be preserved if the Church does not understand and know the power it has as a Standard Bearer of God's Kingdom and lives the Life of Another.

Brokenness is the only method to counteract Satan's objectives. When we are broken, it allows the Power of the Holy Spirit to flow through us, enabling the captive to be set free. When we are broken, faith can rise to the level that will enable us to use the authority given to us by Christ Jesus.

The Internal Cross, self-denial, self-discipline, and death to self, are required if the Church is to fulfill its Mission. When you and I embrace the teachings of the Kingdom of God and God's Grand Plan, there is only one thing we can do. That one thing is to allow the Holy Spirit to have His way with us and to die to the flesh. We must allow our Kingdom Worldview to rule in our heart and mind if we are going complete the Mission given to us and mature into Sonship.

Chapter 3
Accepting the Assignment

Victory (Success) in ministry hinges upon the Call of God. Many have failed because they have entered into their ministry only with good, innocent and noble motives.

THE CALL OF GOD

Let us ask ourselves a few questions if this is true;

1. Can a man or woman initiate his or her own calling?

2. Whom does God call anyway?

3. What are the criteria that God looks for in a man or woman before He calls them?

Paul tells his son in the ministry, Timothy, *"This is a true saying. If a man desires the office of Bishop, he desires a good work."* I Tim 3:1.

It is good that a man or woman desire to meet and fulfill a need to minister to others. However, can they initiate the Call of God to a specific work or position?

In our world today, Humanism is more prevalent then ever before. This humanistic spirit exalts the strength and wisdom of man, making people more man-centered. Our strength of personality, character and disposition along with our academic training with advanced education and degrees causes some men to presume that these God given qualities constitute the call of

God or that these God given qualities qualify them to be called by God to a specific ministry.

Heb 5:1-5 vs. 4, "and no man takes this honor unto himself, but he that is called of God as was Aaron."

Why cannot man take this honor unto himself? One reason is the ministry is God's work not ours. Isaiah understood this when he said, *"Woe is me, for I am undone! Because I am a man of unclean lips, and I dwell in the midst of a people of unclean lips; for my eyes have seen the King, The Lord of hosts." Isa 6:5*

Who of us feels worthy to stand in the place of our Lord and God to speak for Him or minister in His name? No one if he is truly honest. God is sovereign – God alone chooses whomever He will. Only He decides who is to be called, anointed, and placed in positions of leadership. God alone looks, *"not on the outward appearance but the Lord looks on the heart".*

If God does all the choosing in regards to who is called, whom does God call anyway? Who can truly minister the things of the Kingdom except those who are poor in spirit, mourn and are meek? Since God looks on the hearts of those He calls, ministers can be of any age, any occupation, any color/race, or social/economic status.

What does God mean when He says He looks upon the heart – Your Heart? To those who live in the western world – the heart generally means (beside the physical organ) the emotional characteristics of a person. To the Eastern mind (Hebrew), the heart is the core of man's human thoughts, passions, desires, motives affecting purposes, and endeavors. It refers to the personality and inner life and character of an individual.

From the very beginning, we have seen that the Father's desire is to have many sons like His only begotten Son who have a heart like His. The following are some of the Father-heart attitudes of our Lord Jesus Christ:

Willingness: Matt 8:1-3

Forgiveness: Luke 23:34

Concern: Matt 9:11-13

Compassion: Matt 9:35-36

Self-Sacrifice: John 10:15

Humility: Phil 2:5-10

Service: John 13:14

Brokenness: Matt 23:37

Divine Encounter:

Let us suppose that God examines your heart and sees you are a man or women that He will Call. How does God let you know that He has chosen you for a specific ministry? If you look at all the people that God called in the Bible, there is a common thread found. Each of them had a Divine Encounter with God. In each of these, you will see five elements at work: a situation, a command, a prophecy, a promise, and obedience.

Encounters occur while in the presence of God. The Call of God does not come to us second hand. God wants to reveal himself to you so that you will not have any second thoughts or doubts about his Call. As you stand in His presence and His Spirit pulls back the blinders from your eyes, you begin to see that, *"with God ALL things are possible"* and that *His Grace is sufficient for you.* You see clearly, what he has called you to do. Are you practicing "being in" the Presence of God?

Divine Enablement:

Not everyone has been given the same amount of ability, intelligence, patience, quality upbringing, etc, but we all can receive a Divine Enablement to accomplish the task given to us as visualized in the Call. We are all responsible for the use of what we have been given as seen in the parable of the Talents, but that is not a substitute for the Enablement.

It is by God's Grace that we do what we can do. God deposits something within us that without it we would be ineffective. We call that something – The Anointing.

THE ANOINTING - The Anointing is an ability to release the Spirit of God within us, allowing Him to go forth and bring about change in people or situations around us: comfort, encouragement, joy, healing, deliverance, miracles, forgiveness, and the list goes on. The only way people will know that you have been in the presence of God and are called of God, is the Anointing.

The anointing is like gas for a car. We might have a powerhouse for an engine but without gas, we go nowhere. We may have received the power of the Holy Spirit but without the anointing, that power is not transmitted into the spiritual realm where the battle is won. To take dominion and use the power and authority given to us we need the anointing. To be sure, the anointing is not upon us as human beings but upon the word of God within us.

There is a limit to what God can do through us without the Baptism in the Holy Spirit. A builder in this world needs more then a hammer and some nails. Moses, when instructed to build the tabernacle received everything he needed from God- from the plans, to the materials, to the artisans that did the work. To do the work that Christ has given us to do we need the Power of the Holy Spirit.

- *John answered, saying to all," I indeed baptize you with water; but One mightier than I is coming, whose sandal strap I am not worthy to loose. He will baptize you with the Holy Spirit and fire Luke 3:16-17*

- *Behold, I send the Promise of My Father upon you; but tarry in the city of Jerusalem until you are endued with power from on high." Luke 24:49*

- *But you shall receive power when the Holy Spirit has come upon you; and you shall be witnesses to Me in Jerusalem, and in all Judea and Samaria, and to the end of the earth." Acts 1:8*

There is a faith given with the Baptism in the Spirit to use the AUTHORITY that Jesus said we could use. With this one event, Jesus, who was made our Lord and Christ, sweeps aside our weakness, puts a coal from the fire to our lips, and dares man, demons, sickness, poverty, and even death to question our authority.

Either Authority is taken from or it is given to another. Satan deceived and stole the authority that God originally gave to man but Jesus conquered Satan, took back the authority and now returns it to us. This act of power now enables us to wage war against the enemy with His authority. Now that authority (the power to accomplish) is returned to us, God makes us Ambassadors of His Kingdom; therefore, we now can accomplish great things for our Savor King.

And Jesus came and spoke to them, saying, "All authority has been given to Me in heaven and on earth. Go therefore and make disciples of all the nations, baptizing them in the name of the Father and of the Son and of the Holy Spirit, teaching them to observe all things that I have commanded you; and lo, I am with you always, even to the end of the age." Amen. Matt 28:18-20

Divine Preparation:

Be diligent to present yourself approved to God, a worker who does not need to be ashamed, rightly dividing the word of truth. 2 Tim 2:15

Somewhere between God's Call and His anointing there is the process of Preparation. This preparation usually is a multi-step process and is different for each one of us because God has an Individualized Training program in mind.

KINGDOM VISION

Definition: "Vision for ministry is a clear mental image of a preferable future imparted by God to his chosen servants and is based upon an accurate understanding of God, self, and circumstances." George Barna

When a man has received a vision from God, it can be said that he has interpreted the mind of God. So often our hearts groan and cry out, "Oh that the mind of God about the present situation could be recognized by His people that we might have wisdom to impact our world." A vision makes it plain what God desires from and for His people. The problem, for us, in regards to receiving a vision from God, is that the vision usually goes against the prevailing stream of thought in the world and maybe even in the church. Therefore, a battle begins within; the vision either dies or takes on life.

Whatever your personal ambition, it will be changed when you receive a Kingdom vision. You will find yourself running to God, for the vision will always be bigger than you. The vision before Abraham, Moses, and the Apostle Paul humbled them as they looked at the task ahead and their own abilities. The vision given to us will humble us as well. God will at the same time, however let us know that, "all things are possible with God".

Once we know the Mission, are Broken, and then respond to the Call of God, it is now necessary that we receive a Vision. This Vision will put our total being in motion. Our spiritual gifts, our natural talent, our passion, our temperament, our leadership style will all come together and faith, hope and love will find expression.

As we delight in the Lord; as we rejoice in the God of our salvation, as we carry this desire within us, God begins to put flesh on the skeleton of desire and what starts within us as a desire develops and we give birth to a vision.

A vision has no force of its own. It must be imparted to the visionless for it to have an impact. It must be communicated effectively to others so they too can give of themselves and have a part in its fulfillment. This is where most fail.

People will respond to a charismatic leader and follow him. If, however, they have not received and bought into his vision, the work will stop, and the ministry will end.

Vision is not about the status quo of today. Vision involves change. It requires stepping out of your comfort zone. If you have a vision it will cause you to focus in on your work, cause you to exert control over your environment and be driven to shape the future.

A vision is for the future. It involves change. Because no one naturally likes change, it is not difficult for Satan to stir up resentment, murmurings, and complaining as Moses found out. If God has given you a vision, you must be committed to the vision and keep the rewards of realization before the people that are following you and who are to come after.

Satan will make every effort to keep us from receiving a vision.

1. He knows that having a vision will keep us going in the heat of the battle.
2. He knows that vision produces risk takers.
3. He knows that a vision will inspire strategies, goals, and plans.
4. He knows that a vision will fuel enthusiasm.
5. He knows that with a vision comes: creativity, faith, inventiveness, hope, loyalty, dedication, devotion, responsibility, accountability, self-discipline, determination, commitment, steadfastness, persistence, and hard work.

Everything we do in ministry must relate to the mission and to the vision God gives to us. If not we will be spinning our wheels doing those things that will not fulfill our purpose.

Then Jesus answered and said to them, "Most assuredly, I say to you, the Son can do nothing of Himself, but what He sees the Father do; for whatever He does, the Son also does in like manner. For the Father loves the Son, and shows Him all things that He Himself does; and He will show Him greater works than these, that you may marvel." John 5:19-20

The above text implies that the Father reveals what Jesus was to do. Jesus knew His mission and had before Him a vision of what He was to do. His mission was to re-establish the Father's Kingdom and to build His Church. His vision showed Him how He was to accomplish His work.

He invited those 1st Century Disciples into the Kingdom that they might receive all the benefits of the Kingdom. He made it known that He was the door - the way into the Kingdom. Jesus went about teaching in their synagogues, preaching the Gospel of the Kingdom, and healing all kinds of sickness and all kinds of disease among the people. He was giving them a vision of the Kingdom that they could enter, not when they died, but right then. He gave His Apostles a vision that might thrust into ministry after they were filled with the Holy Spirit.

Transformation occurs by the operation of the Holy Spirit within us. It is through this ongoing relationship with the Holy Spirit that vision is also imparted. God, by His Spirit, reveals things directly into our spirit, which our natural eyes and ears can never sense. When this occurs, Paul says, *"we are led by the spirit".*

VALUES: As a vision will give direction to your mission, values will guide your behavior and determine how you will perform your labor to accomplish your vision. These values reflect not only what is important to us but reveal the lengths we will go to in order to protect our culture. If you change a culture's values, you change its culture. These values determine where we will invest our time, money, and our heart.

The values of a culture soon become it laws for all to follow, whether oral or written. In the culture of the Kingdom, the Ten Commandments are at the very center of its value system. People of like values are drawn to each other, however when our God given values are shown to the world they are drawn to us because they are something to be admired.

Every person and every organization has core values. Until you identify and confidently state your values, Satan will try to fill your heart with other lesser values that will pollute your mission and throw you off course.

Your values will filter your decisions and your use of your resources. They will keep you when times get tough. The will keep you on the high road, that narrow way, the straight path.

They will be the tool that you will hold others accountable that catch your vision and come along side of you. Core values tie its members together in UNITY. People can have the same vision but if they have widely different values, they will be torn apart.

The Sermon on the Mount is Jesus' statement of the values of the Kingdom of God. As an example, He says, *"You have heard that it was said to those of old, 'You shall not murder, and whoever murders will be in danger of the judgment.' But I say to you...".* He sets a higher standard of values for His disciples.

God's desire for His Church is to come into a place of community. The Community's values are what drive and motivate what we define as the core beliefs we are passionate about and how we measure our goals and priorities. Each local church and ministry needs to define its core community and leadership values.

CORE COMMUNITY VALUES of KINGDOM COMMUNITY CHURCH INTERNATIONAL

Purpose is Primary

Purpose is defined as the reason for which something is done or something exists. Bobb Biehl likes to say, "Without an accurate answer to the question 'why,' the price will always be too high." We believe that is true. Therefore, as a community, we seek the root causes and universal principles that make our lives work so that we may live intentionally and create sustainable outcomes.

Community is Catalyzing

Community is made up of two words, common and unity. Where there is unity there is an opportunity for transformation in the hearts of those who are unified. Transformation is primarily experiential and relational, not informational. Therefore, we believe that the assembly of the body of Christ is not only essential but extremely rewarding as we strive to discover and develop our full potential. As a community, we seek to accelerate one another's process of growth by offering our authentic selves in loving relationships of support, encouragement, and accountability.

Benevolence is Beneficial

Benevolence is defined in the dictionary as service of a charitable rather than profit-making purpose. But in the Kingdom, Jesus defined acts of service and charity towards others as a profitable exchange in favor of the servant. In fact, He Himself lived a life of service to others and modeled the investment mentality He wanted us, His followers, to adopt. No good deed or contribution goes unnoticed in the Kingdom because "it is more blessed to give than to receive." We sow seed expecting to reap a harvest in kind. As a community, we seek to be known and defined as a generous people.

Whole is the Goal

As human beings, we are three parts: spirit, soul, and body. If we tend to one part while ignoring the others, or tend to the immaterial while ignoring the material, then we are presenting an incongruent message to others that wars against our core design. For too long, the church has focused solely on the immaterial "soul" while vilifying the material "flesh" to the detriment of its followers. The Bible, however, never demonizes the material parts of our world - God created them, after all - but gives us a mandate of responsibility to our physical environments and ourselves. In our community, we seek to become whole (healed, healthy, peaceful) people by aligning all parts of our being - spirit, soul, and body - with the lifestyle of the Kingdom to be a model to our world.

Joy is in the Journey

Jesus never gave an overview or a 5-year plan to his disciples when He commissioned them for service. "Follow Me," is all they ever heard before beginning their journey with Him. We, too, have been asked to follow the Lord as He leads us throughout our lives. Knowing where we are going is a certainty we don't always receive. In our community, we learn to love the process of transformation that we are all involved in and take joy in obeying the Lord's voice, even if we don't always know exactly where we're going.

THE

TEN COMMANDMENTS

And the Lord spoke all these words, saying: I am the Lord thy God, who brought you out of the land of Egypt, out of the house of bondage. Exodus 20:1-17(LXX)

I. Thou shall have no other gods beside me.

II. Thou shall not make to thyself an idol, nor likeness of anything, whatever things are in the heaven above, and whatever are in the earth beneath, and whatever are in the waters under the earth. Thou shall not bow down to them, nor serve them; for I am the Lord thy God, a jealous God, recompensing the sins of the fathers upon the children, to the third and fourth generation to them that hate me, and bestowing mercy on them that love me to thousands of them, and on them that keep my commandments.

III. Thou shall not take the name of the Lord thy God in vain; for the Lord thy God will not acquit him that takes his name in vain.

IV. Remember the Sabbath day to keep it holy. Six days thou shall labor, and shall perform all thy work. But on the seventh day is the Sabbath of the Lord thy God; on it thou shall do no work, thou, nor thy son, nor thy daughter, thy servant nor thy maidservant, your ox nor your donkey nor any cattle of your, nor the stranger that sojourns with thee. For in six days the Lord made the heaven and the earth, and the sea and all things in them, and rested on the seventh

61

day; therefore, the Lord blessed the seventh day, and hallowed it.

V. Honor thy father and thy mother, that it may be well with thee, and that thou may live long on the good land, which the Lord thy God gives to thee.

VI. Thou shall not commit adultery.

VII. Thou shall not steal.

VIII. Thou shall not kill.

IX. Thou shall not bear false witness against thy neighbor.

X. Thou shall not covet thy neighbor's wife; thou shall not covet thy neighbor's house; nor his field, nor his servant, nor his maid, nor his ox, nor his donkey, nor any of his cattle, nor whatever belongs to thy neighbors.

Chapter 4
The Heart of The Minister:
Part I

In the last two Chapters, we looked at Ministry - The Preparation. Before we look at Ministry in Action, we need to look at The Heart of the Minister. The early Church turned their world upside down and we can turn our world up side down also but it involves knowing what is in our heart. What is in our heart will reflect the Culture of the Kingdom that we have accepted. Faith must be an active ingredient in our culture.

ACCORDING TO YOUR FAITH

What does it profit, my brethren, if someone says he has faith but does not have works? Can faith save him? What does it profit, my brethren, if someone says he has faith but does not have works? Can faith save him? If a brother or sister is naked and destitute of daily food, and one of you says to them, "Depart in peace, be warmed and filled," but you do not give them the things which are needed for the body, what does it profit? Thus also faith by itself, if it does not have works, is dead. But someone will say, "You have faith, and I have works." Show me your faith without your works, and I will show you my faith by my works. You believe that there is one God. You do well. Even the demons believe — and tremble! But do you want to know, O foolish man, that faith without works is dead? James 2:14, 16-20

We know that Faith is important. In the early days of the Charismatic movement, a multitude of books were written to help us to understand Faith, however, we seem to be no better off than before. We have for so long tried to study, define, dissect or look into the meaning of Faith but without providing God's people a life of living by Faith. Nevertheless, we will try to bring about a clear perception of Faith.

Let us start with a personal experience that has served me well for over 36 years. In January 1974, God gave to me a vision of a house filled, with my not only three boys but also foster children. This was something that neither my wife nor I had even thought about much less discussed. However, my first thought was to talk to my pastor and seek his wisdom. After I explained to him the vision, and what God had said, he too thought it was from God. He advised me not to be discouraged if I encountered set backs but to continue until the vision became a reality.

There were several things to be considered. The first thing was my family had to be in agreement to move forward. The second was that we had only $10.00 in our savings.

To say that I was a little overwhelmed would have been an understatement to say the least. I needed Faith. As I thought about this, I began to look back since the time I gave my life to Christ to see what He had done in my life and the Faith that I already demonstrated. What I saw was that over the seven months since my conversion, God had given me many situations where my Faith had a chance to grow. I realized that growth in Faith is progressive and that God never asked me to do anything that I did not have Faith for. Therefore, that which God was asking me to do now was not above my Faith level or above the level He was leading us to.

The secret that I learned is this; IT IS ALL ABOUT RELATIONSHIP. The depth of our relationship will determine the depth of our Faith. What determines the depth of our relationship is INVOLVEMENT. We must be involved with the other person, whether it is our children, wife, friend, mother, father or GOD.

As I talked with my heavenly father, three words kept swirling around in my head, CONFIDENCE, TRUST AND ASSURANCE. As we continued in our talk, He said, "put them in this order; assurance, confidence then trust. Now use the first letter of each word and see what it spells-ACT." As I thought about what He said, it all began to make sense.

Let me explain. I began by reviewing what I knew about these three words and how they might relate to what I knew about God. I will review only a few things because you need to do this on your own.

ASSURANCE: I knew that God never lied to me. He always kept His promises. His oath was His bond. I knew that He always kept His word. Because of my involvement with my wife of 48 years, I know she has never lied to me, has always kept her promises to me and our boys, and could be depended upon to keep her word. I had an assurance in her pledge to us. It is the same with God.

CONFIDENCE: Just as I needed certainty in my Worldview in order to have peace within, I had a conviction that which God had started He would complete. When I hired someone to work on my car and they did a good job, at a fair price, confidence in them resulted. When I saw that they never waivered in the work ethic, I had confidence to return and recommend them to my friends. It was the same with God.

TRUST: When I've been unemployed, when my parents and son died, when other destructive situations came my way, God was always there. He has been my rock, my fortress and my deliverer. I know that whatever the circumstance I can trust in the love of God. He has never left me nor forsaken me in 37 years. Through it all my sister, Marilyn has been there. We have more them a relationship, we have been involved with each other's lives. My wife, Bea, has that same involvement with her five brothers; when the chips are down, she can turn to them. It is the same with God.

When we have, through experience, ASSURANCE, CONFIDENCE AND TRUST IN OUR GOD, Faith is a natural outcome and we ACT. It becomes a way of life, Abundant Life.

FAITH:

But without faith it is impossible to please Him, for he who comes to God must believe that He is, and that He is a rewarder of those who diligently seek Him. Heb 11:6

The above Scripture is foundational to receive anything from God. It is essential then that we understand its definition as given in *Heb 11:1-2; "Now faith is the substance of things hoped for, the evidence of things not seen".*

Evidence: Evidence is proof that enables you and me to come to a particular conclusion. In a courtroom, both sides present evidence to prove their case. The jury listens to both sides and then decides who is telling the truth and who isn't. Our actions prove what we believe is the truth. However, in the court of Heaven, only the truth that corresponds with the truth of God's Word will carry any weight.

When we go before God with our need, Satan will be there to present his evidence that will prevent your answer from coming your way. The evidence you and I bring is our Faith. It is by "according to your faith will it be unto you". It is by Faith that salvation, healing, provision or deliverance come from the spiritual realm to the physical realm.

Historically, Biblical Faith is seen as a belief or mental assent to some truth or as a person's basic orientation. Faith is best described as trust, confidence or loyalty. Both of these definitions are inadequate, as neither takes into account the vital part in the process of hearing God's Word because *"faith comes by hearing, and hearing by the word of God."*

Someone has defined Faith as involving three essential elements: <u>knowledge</u>, <u>agreement</u>, and <u>trust</u> (the working of faith). One cannot have agreement and trust without knowledge of that with which he agrees and trusts.

A person cannot be saved until he hears the gospel, which is both the Word of God and the will of God. When he hears the Word, then, and only then does he have a basis to believe. When he believes, he will repent and will allow the Holy Spirit to transform him. Hence, his Faith is seen.

The new Believer's Faith is the evidence of the thing hoped for. We have Hope because the Word we read and mediate on is the truth. It is the truth that gives us Hope. Hope and truth go together. Hope just doesn't appear. Hope is based on the truth of God's Word. We understand then, that there is great difference between hope and Faith. Faith is present and Hope (the sure Word of God that will not return to Him void) is future. Faith is active while Hope is passive. Faith is not faith when substance can be seen, and Hope is not Hope when realized.

Hope deals with the psychological and deep feelings of man while faith deals with the spirit of man. Hope keeps us from being fearful as we face the struggles and pains of life. Faith gives us the assurance and confidence knowing in the end we shall receive that which we have hoped.

Putting Faith and Hope together

When we have a need, the answer is first in the spiritual realm before it appears in the physical realm. Let us say that our need is financial due to added family responsibilities; not because we want a flat screen TV or a new car. Therefore, we go to God's Word (truth) and seek God. Yes, seek God. He says draw near to me and I will draw near to you. He says call to me and I will answer you, and show you great and mighty things, which you do not know.

We must have an encounter with God. It is not just a matter of finding some scripture and confessing it over and over that brings the answer. It is not confession that brings possession. It is encountering God and listening as He speaks to us from His Word.

In the context of God's love, the Scriptures we have been meditating on, give us hope for the answer to our need. A vision forms in our spirit and Hope springs up in our heart and soul. Joy enters in and this is what keeps us from depression and being fearful, no matter how bad things get.

A KINGDOM WHICH CANNOT BE SHAKEN

Hope is hope, it is not Faith; we must not get confused between the two. Hope does not bring the answer into the physical realm, faith does.

After our encounter with God, we must continue searching Scripture (truth) in order for God to show us those great and mighty things, which we do not know. As we do, there comes a moment when we hear the still small voice of the Spirit of God say, "this is the way walk in it". A specific Scripture comes alive and we know that God has heard our prayer.

There are times when this happens that we know that we know our prayer is answered. In other words, it's a done deal. There are other times, when Faith has come, but there seems to be a little doubt, we are a little hesitant. Faith and doubt cannot exist together and if they do, you cannot receive the answer.

How do you get rid of the doubt so that Faith can have its way? You begin by confessing to God what He has said to you earlier. Over and over, you remind God what He has said and that you trust Him to perform His word. This is not confession bringing possession, it is GROWING YOUR FAITH.

Let me try to explain through a hypothetical situation. Across America, people are losing their jobs because of the recession and you are one of them. You were told that God would take care of His family so you seek Him out in His Word (truth), looking for His promises. You find that, as you are searching The Word, something is happening to you; Hope is beginning to rise up with you. That much-needed job, which seemed so far away, now seems closer and a real possibility. Now that we have Hope, we need to continue on in order to receive Faith that the job might become a reality.

On a sheet of paper, let us draw a stickman on the left side of the page that represents, you. On the right side of the page, draw something that represents the kind of work you are looking for. Now draw a vertical line down the middle of the page that separates the two. The space on the left represents the physical realm and the space on the right represents the spiritual realm.

68

Draw a line from (you) with an arrow at the end, pointing to the picture of the job you want. This line represents the HOPE that you now have (because of the truth of God's Word). You have now crossed over from the physical to the spiritual. WOW- that is exciting but you still need FAITH to bring your job from the spiritual into the physical so you can go to work and make some money.

Draw another line from you to the job, but this time put a hook on the end. As your faith increases, you will be pulling the job closer and closer to you. It is your Faith that reaches out into the spiritual realm and takes hold of what you need.

Knowing that you need FAITH in order to receive the job, you continue seeking God in His Word. Here is what will happen: you will encounter God and He will give a personal Word to you. A specific Scripture will jump out at you and you will begin to confess this promise over and over. This confessing is just as much a prayer as when you first lost your job and you were asking God for help. As you repeat God's promise to you, it is mixed with thanksgiving and your Faith increases and the reality of the job comes closer and closer as if the picture you have drawn on the paper is moving across the page to the left side to your picture.

Use the WORKSHEET AT END OF BOOK for your own needs

"In this you greatly rejoice, though now for a little while, if need be, you have been grieved by various trials, that the genuineness of your faith, being much more precious than gold that perishes, though it is tested by fire, may be found to praise, honor, and glory at the revelation of Jesus Christ, whom having not seen you love. Though now you do not see Him, yet believing, you rejoice with joy inexpressible and full of glory, receiving the end of your faith, the salvation of your souls. 1 Peter 1:6-9.

When Faith arises and increases within you, there is something real happening in you. You have no doubt, no fear, and no anxiousness because you know that you will soon have the job and be able to support your self and others. In fact, you have the job already in the spiritual realm, it is just waiting for you to come and apply.

Here's the Point – the promises of God first have fulfillment in the spiritual realm before they are manifested in the physical realm. This is why we begin with the Word of God and not prayer. We want answers in the physical but we must begin knowing the will of God and His promises.

When Abram was 90 years old, God spoke to him and said that he would have a child. His wife Sarah was well past the age of child bearing, yet Abram believed God. He began to speak his new name: Abraham. He went out at age 90 and told everyone that God had given him a new name, a name that meant father of many.

Peter had called Jesus' attention to the Fig tree, and Jesus responded, *"Have faith in God"*. Here is what happened: the day before Jesus spoke the Word of God to the tree. Nothing happened immediately that could be seen physically. However, Jesus was using the same faith principle He was teaching his disciples to use – He *was "calling things that were not as though they were"*. His faith was the substance of what He hoped would be. By morning, the physical had caught up with the spiritual and the tree was dead. Jesus then said, *"For assuredly, I say to you, whoever says to this mountain, 'Be removed and be cast into the sea,' and does not doubt in his heart, but believes that those things he says will be done, he will have whatever he says. Therefore I say to you, whatever things you ask when you pray, believe that you receive them, and you will have them." Mark 11:23-24*

Faith is more then believing. Faith is going forward on **trust**. We can believe in many things but it is not until we put that belief to the test will we find out if our faith is real and genuine. Faith is **confidence** based on witness of past performance. Faith is **assurance** that the person who made the promise will fulfill their word or contract.

PREDETERMINISM

Since ministry is making right what Satan has made wrong, Satan does not want us to know the benefits of being a citizen of the Kingdom nor does he want us to share them with others. He will make use of every advantage in order to hinder our faith, preventing us from receiving these benefits for ourselves and taking them to others.

If, in our Worldview we conclude that God is Omnipotent and therefore all things are possible with God; then why are not all healed, delivered, redeemed or whatever else we might be praying for? The answer might be found in a Biblical Worldview that includes a belief in Predeterminism.

PREDETERMINISM, as it relates to Faith, is the doctrine or belief that God causes everything and He not only knows and ordains all that happens, but that He is involved in and determines all that happens, down to the smallest detail. It also enlists the thought of the Sovereignty of God, whereby we assign to Him independence in deciding what is best for each individual and therefore brings it about.

We learned in our study of Worldviews, you cannot believe in two conflicting points of view at the same time and maintain peace within. Therefore, concerning healing; if one believes that it is always God's will to heal and yet also believes in Predeterminism; a conflict will arise because these two positions are diametrically opposed to each other. They both "cannot fit within the same jellybean jar". It is impossible to have biblical Faith in healing if you do not believe that healing falls under God's intentional will for you personally.

The question is: can there be an understanding of the providence and sovereignty of God, which allows for human freedom?" We have already looked at this concept of freedom but it still can be troublesome for those who believe in Predeterminism. One of the attributes of God is Omniscience or foreknowledge. If you understand this term as God having a perfect way of knowing, then there is no theological dilemma. However, if God knows the future because He determines it, foreordains and wills it then what can be said of human freedom? What can be said of Faith?

Since God is All Powerful, meaning He can do anything and if we believe in Predeterminism, that God foreordains the future, does that mean that God will do whatever He wants? Does His Sovereignty hold a person back from having the Faith to be healed or receiving anything else that is asked for?

Jerry Simmons, in his book, "THAT THEY MAY KNOW" says, "If God is using His Power to direct the affairs of men what does that say of the power of His Love? Since God's desire is for each individual to love Him willingly and to give willingly, any activity of God that denies or suppresses man's volition would defeat His purpose. His use of power or sovereignty then would be a confession of weakness and an acceptance of defeat."

We can believe in the omnipotence, the providence of God and the sovereignty of God without believing that He determines every action and event. We can do so because, He limits Himself by His own decrees to certain spiritual laws that He himself will not break.

Here is an example of the above: The penalty for Sin and the "whosoever" of the atonement. God declared that the penalty of sin is death. Since we all have sinned, spiritual death has come to all. God could have withdrawn his Word but if he had, He would not have been true to His own law. God had to come up with a solution if He was going to keep His Promise to reclaim and re-establish His Kingdom. God had to find a way to redeem and justify humanity within the limits that He had set for himself.

Before the foundation of the earth, God had prepared a way to satisfy both the demands of the law and the performance of His Word. He accomplished both by having His Word become flesh. His Word became Jesus, who died on the cross, satisfied the justice of the Father, rose from the grave, and destroyed the power that Satan had over man.

God's acceptance of the atonement for all who have sinned, allows for the "whosoever" to accept or reject the forgiveness offered. God knows all who will accept or reject His grace, but that does not mean that He foreordained or predetermined that decision.

For those participating in Kingdom Building, we must conclude that God does not predetermine sickness, disease, loss of employment, accidents or anything else evil as His Will for anybody. To the contrary, Jesus came to give Life and Life abundant. Satan has come to steal, kill and destroy.

So why does man then find the need to believe in the absolute sovereignty of God? The answer is simple; they have no answers for man's troubles or the Faith required for the need presented. For an answer to this dilemma, refer back to Chapter 2 of, BORN TO RULE", regarding Economics. Through my waiting upon the Lord, I have come to believe that God's Sovereignty has more to do with His timing of what He does, than controlling the affairs of Man.

GOD'S ANSWERS FOR HUMANITY ARE NOT FOUND IN THIS WORLD. THEY ARE FOUND IN THE SPIRITUAL WORLD. JESUS SAID, "MY KINGDOM IS NOT OF THIS WORLD." GOD'S ANSWERS ARE FOUND IN HIS KINGDOM WHERE HE SITS ON HIS THRONE. WE ARE SPIRIT BEINGS AND NOTHING CAN NOW STOP US FROM COMING BEFORE GOD. WE CAN COME BOLDLY INTO HIS KINGDOM, UNTO HIS THRONE, TO RECEIVE MERCY AND GRACE FOR ALL OUR NEEDS.

OUR PROBLEM IS IN NOT KNOWING HOW TO TRANSFER OUR MIND FROM THIS WORLD TO THE OTHER. GOD HAS PROVIDED THE WAY INTO HIS KINGDOM AND HIS PRESENCE THROUGH WORSHIP. IT IS WHEN WE SET ALL ELSE ASIDE AND ENTER INTO HIS PRESENCE THAT WE SEE THE ANSWER TO OUR NEED AND THE NEEDS OF OTHERS. IT IS BY FAITH THAT WE BRING HIS ANSWER BACK INTO THE PHYSICAL REALM.

THE PRACTICALITY OF FASTING

Much has been said regarding, "Practicing the Presence of God". There is no surer way than that of FASTING to enter into the presence of God. If you are a backslider, a lukewarm Christian, a Christian in need of wisdom or a miracle, nothing can bring you back quicker into the presence of God then fasting.

It is interesting that the word FAST first appears in Scripture admonishing the Israelites to hold "fast" (stay close) to the Lord. While the first time that the word "fast" (absences from food) is used, it is when just the opposite had occurred, when David committed adultery and his son is dying.

So Why Fast? Paul uses one-half of Romans 8 to tell us why we are lacking in power for righteous living and are ineffective in ministry. Sin comes through the appetites of the flesh. Therefore, Paul is not talking here about flesh and blood, but of the man that lives as if there is no God and as if he is not accountable to anyone but himself.

When Paul says that we must die daily, he is not talking about physical death. He is telling us that we must not give in to the old self (natural man) that wants to live as if there is no God to which he is accountable.

The "natural" man wants its own way and wants to forget that he has entered into a covenant relationship. The Holy Spirit wants to remind him but the natural man quenches the Holy Spirit. The Spirit within, however, would lead us in the path of righteousness, that we might walk with God. We can trust in ourselves or we can trust in God. Paul says, "Let no flesh glory before God" as Paul does not want to glory in anything except in Christ.

Another aspect of the flesh (natural man) is similar to the response of a defiant, strong willed child, "I can do it myself." Jeremiah contrasts the two types of trust that are available to man.

"Cursed is the man who trusts in man and makes flesh his strength, whose heart departs from the Lord. Jer 17:5

"Blessed is the man who trusts in the lord, and whose hope is in the Lord". Jer 17:7

Both, trusting in the "natural man" and then letting the flesh have its own way; will stop us from being effective in ministry. The "natural man" blocks out the power for ministry. How can we get back on track and back into fellowship?

Jesus tells the people gathered at the Sermon on the Mount, *"Blessed are they that hunger and thirst for righteousness for they shall be filled"*; here we have cause and effect. When we are hungry, it says we are in need, therefore, it moves us to action. The action Jesus is referring to is SEEKING for what is needed.

Fasting is about seeking. We know that, *"God rewards those that diligently seek Him".* Therefore, we seek God because nothing else will satisfy the desire within us. It means walking in the light as He is in the light. It means purging ourselves of all that will hinder the process. It means refusing to compromise and accept less that which is sought after. It means having focus.

Fasting means seeking after that which we hold in high esteem, highly value and which we deem indispensable. It means we will sacrifice all else to obtain that which we are seeking. We will sacrifice not only food but also TV, social events and even intimate relationships with our spouse.

We seek God not because He is hiding from us. We seek Him because He is found in the spiritual realm, not the physical. It is when we make a thoughtful resolution to pursue God that we will be rewarded - *"draw near to God and He will draw near to you".*

Fasting diminishes the power of the flesh and allows the Holy Spirit to speak to our spirit. Fasting allows us to be more aware of Jesus, who has given us authority to use His Name and minister to others.

TRIALS AND ADVERSITY - Trials can either make us or break us. They will cause us to face our need for Jesus or they will cause us to look to the natural man. We will look for wisdom from God or look for wisdom from the world. If we are desperate (poor in spirit) we will fast and seek the Lord. When we seek the Lord, we will find him.

Living Sacrifice - We must take Paul's admonishment to us seriously. *"I beseech you therefore, brethren, by the mercies of God, that you present your bodies a living sacrifice, holy, acceptable to God, which is your reasonable service. And do not be conformed to this world, but be transformed by the renewing of your mind, that you may prove what is that good and acceptable and perfect will of God."* Rom 12:1-2

Paul's admonishment is for our whole self to be involved in this sacrifice. Paul always puts the spirit first except here because here the body is all-inclusive. He is speaking of our total being, including our spirit and soul as well as our bodies to be involved.

Our desire, as ministers, should be to have access to the Holy Spirit. Jesus said that we should take up our cross and follow Him. Here Paul says that we should offer our bodies as a living sacrifice. When we consider ourselves *crucified with Christ; it is no longer we, who live, but Christ who lives in us; and the life which we now live in the flesh (natural man) we live by faith in the Son of God, who loved us and gave Himself for us.*

David felt his emptiness of the Holy Spirit and cries out in Psalm 51, *"Create in me a clean heart Oh God and renew a right spirit within and take not thy Holy Spirit from me."* David feels this way because he knows that it is, *"Not by might nor by power, but by My Spirit, Says the Lord of hosts"* that will keep him in his position as King of Israel.

RENEWAL – Our days are so busy, we need frequent touches of God's presence and power. No Christian is immune from this need for a renewed experience with our heavenly Father. Many activities and pressures often distract us. Therefore, we are not mindful of his presence every day. It is as if we are walking deeper and deeper into the forest, losing our way; having lost our compass. It is usually when we have exhausted our human resources that we give up and cry out in desperation.

Without this reliance on God's power, we will be doomed to live lives that are wallowing in mediocrity, never knowing the full joy of the Lord. We often want to enjoy the presence of God without participation in the fasting and prayer that brings the presence.

Examples of the practical practice of fasting:

2 Chron 20:2-3 Then some came and told Jehoshaphat, saying, "A great multitude is coming against you from beyond the sea, from Syria; and they are in Hazazon Tamar" (which is En Gedi).And Jehoshaphat feared, and set himself to seek the Lord, and proclaimed a fast throughout all Judah. So Judah gathered together to ask help from the Lord; and from all the cities of Judah they came to seek the Lord. Read through verse 17

Ezra 8:21-23 Then I proclaimed a fast there at the river of Ahava, that we might humble ourselves before our God, to seek from Him the right way for us and our little ones and all our possessions. For I was ashamed to request of the king an escort of soldiers and horsemen to help us against the enemy on the road, because we had spoken to the king, saying, "The hand of our God is upon all those for good who seek Him, but His power and His wrath are against all those who forsake Him." So we fasted and entreated our God for this, and He answered our prayer.

TUE TURUST OF COMPASSION

The Bible gives us a beautiful picture of compassion when it tells the story of Moses going up Mount Abarim to look at the Promised Land. Moses, however, is held back from going in because of his own rebellion. Even though Moses is prevented from going into the Promised Land, he is not concerned with his own self but God's people. He knows someone must take his place; someone with the same heart of compassion for God's people, a leader with a heart of a Shepherd.

Then Moses spoke to the Lord, saying: "Let the Lord, the God of the spirits of all flesh, set a man over the congregation, who may go out before them and go in before them, who may lead them out and bring them in, that the congregation of the Lord may not be like sheep which have no shepherd." Num 27:15-17

Later in Israel's history when David is made King, they see in him the heart of compassion. In David; they see a contrast from King Saul.

Then all the tribes of Israel came to David at Hebron and spoke, saying, "Indeed we are your bone and your flesh. Also, in time past, when Saul was king over us, you were the one who led Israel out and brought them in; and the Lord said to you,' You shall shepherd My people Israel, and be ruler over Israel.'" 2 Sam 5:1-3

Although many titles are given to God's leaders and ministers, the title of **Shepherd** is used the least. I think the reason for this is that most leaders have not fully experienced or practiced true shepherding. They have become administrators.

God looked down on the people in Ezekiel's day; A day (season) when there was no shepherd for God's people.

And the word of the Lord came to me, saying, "Son of man, prophesy against the shepherds of Israel, prophesy and say to them, 'Thus says the Lord God to the shepherds: "Woe to the shepherds of Israel who feed themselves! Should not the shepherds feed the flocks? You eat the fat and clothe yourselves with the wool; you slaughter the fatlings, but you do not feed the flock. The weak you have not strengthened, nor have you healed those who were sick, nor bound up the broken, nor brought back hat was driven away, nor sought what was lost; but with force and cruelty you have ruled them. So they were scattered because there was no shepherd; and they became food for all the beasts of the field when they were scattered. My sheep wandered through all the mountains, and on every high hill; yes, My flock was scattered over the whole face of the earth, and no one was seeking or searching for them." Ezek 34:1-6

God wanted to know, where are the shepherds? We have people in the church today that want to "minister". This title, however, does not reveal any distinction between a true servant of God and a man or women who falsely wears the title. We can be a part of the prayer ministry, the children's ministry, the men's or women's ministry or even be ordained as part of the professional 'Ministry' and still not do the spiritual work of the church. It is no wonder that God's people are weak and sickly.

Compassion is at the heart of the true shepherd. We should see the word Compassion as interwoven into the actions of everyone who wants to shepherd or minister to others. Having compassion goes way beyond being kind, showing goodness, or feeling sorry for someone. This can all be superficial and produce little or no action on the part of the observer. We all want to do something to help a little child or the cripple but should a tragedy occur to an able body man or women; then that is another story. We seem to pick and chose who will receive our compassion.

Everyone who wants to fulfill his or her responsibility in the Kingdom of God must have the heart qualifications of a shepherd. In other words, they must have Compassion.

In the Old Testament, Jehovah is the Great Shepherd. In the New Testament, Jesus is the Good Shepherd. Nothing shows the heart of Jesus so beautifully as: *Mark 6:33-35*

78

But the multitudes saw them departing, and many knew Him and ran there on foot from all the cities. They arrived before them and came together to Him. And Jesus, when He came out, saw a great multitude and was moved with compassion for them, because they were like sheep not having a shepherd. So He began to teach them many things.

This word Compassion expresses the instinctive attachment of one being to another. It has it seat in the maternal bosom; *Then the woman whose son was living spoke to the king, for she yearned with compassion for her son; and she said, "O my lord, give her the living child, and by no means kill him!" But the other said, "Let him be neither mine nor yours, but divide him." So the king answered and said, "Give the first woman the living child, and by no means kill him; she is his mother." 1 Kings 3:26-27 And* in the heart of a father; *"As a father pities his children, So the Lord pities those who fear Him. For He knows our frame; He remembers that we are dust." Ps 103:13-14*

People all around us are in shambles and in need of love and compassion. There are so many that are broken-hearted, hurt, disillusioned, abandoned and in need of someone who can provide some solutions to their problems.

Jesus tells the parable of the Good Samaritan that reveals Compassion in action: *"Then Jesus answered and said, "A certain man went down from Jerusalem to Jericho, and fell among thieves, who stripped him of his clothing, wounded him, and departed, leaving him half dead. Now by chance a certain priest came down that road. And when he saw him, he passed by on the other side"*

Likewise, a Levite, when he arrived at the place, came and looked, and passed by on the other side. But a certain Samaritan, as he journeyed, came where he was. And when he saw him, he had compassion. So he went to him and bandaged his wounds, pouring on oil and wine; and he set him on his own animal, brought him to an inn, and took care of him. On the next day, when he departed, he took out two denarii, gave them to the innkeeper, and said to him, 'Take care of him; and whatever more you spend, when I come again, I will repay you.' So which of these three do you think was neighbor to him who fell among the thieves?" And he said, "He who showed mercy on him." Then Jesus said to him, "Go and do likewise." Luke 10:30-37

This Samaritan was not out looking to do some good; he just stumbled across a man in need. He could have walked on by, nobody would have found fault with him if he had. After all, the Samaritans had nothing to do with Jews. He was on a journey and probably wanted to get to his destination as quickly as possible. In order to meet this man's need, it was going to take much more than just reaching into his pocket to give this man a coin or two.

It would take more then just cleaning his wounds and bandaging him up. He was going to have to give much more than that. He must give up his feelings against the Jews. He must give of his time, his money, his comfort. He must give of himself in order to meet the needs of this stranger. He would have to give of himself for someone who might not do the same for him if the roles where reversed.

If he told this story to his friends, fellow Samaritans, they would most likely ridicule and maybe cast him out for abetting a Jew. He was willing to take that risk, but not only that, he was also willing to follow through by coming back and paying more for this Jew's healing if needed. His compassion thrust him into action.

In Psalm 23, we see the shepherd leading and guiding his sheep to a place where they can feed, find water and comfort so that they would lack nothing. Whatever fears they might have had are now gone. He makes them to understand that following him is the right thing to do.

He disciplines them; they know what the boundaries are and the hurt they will experience when they go off on their own. They know that he will never leave them nor forsake them. He will be there to protect them and fight off their enemies. They rejoice in the fact that when he is there, they are at peace.

The shepherd has compassion on them because sheep are dumb. They are defenseless. They are incapable of fending for themselves. They are lost without a shepherd. If we are to minister to a lost world or even to our brothers and sisters, who have not yet matured in the faith, we must be filled with compassion.

Chapter 5
The Heart of The Minister:
Part 2

Ministry to those in need begins with Prayer. Our Prayers create an atmosphere for change. Prayer is the means to bring God's Kingdom to manifestation in this world because God does everything through prayer.

THE POWER OF PRAYER

In order for God to operate in the physical realm, God needs a physical body. In regards to Jesus, the writer of Hebrews said, *"Therefore, when He came into the world, "Sacrifice and offering you did not desire, but a body you have prepared for me."* We too are the body of Christ and because we have within us the abiding Holy Spirit, God can effect change in this world through us.

Prayer is more than a spiritual exercise; it is the only method that God instituted enabling Him to communicate with those in His family. The Holy Spirit, who abides within you, energizes your spirit. Your spirit has as its first priority, to pray, therefore, it cries out to pray. You are a new creation, which means that your spirit has a Kingdom Connection. Because you have a regenerated spirit, your Heavenly Father now has an earthly connection.

Prayer involves more than asking God for something; there are at least six different aspects.

Nothing helps us to center on God better than giving thanks. THANKSGIVING brings to mind all that God has done for us and for others in a specific area (deliverance from drugs, healing of cancer, etc.). Thanksgiving, just by its very nature, causes us to bring forth PRAISE to our God who is all-powerful, is all-knowing, and who demonstrates His love to us. There is nothing like standing in the presence of a holy God to make us fall on our face, CONFESS our sins, and seek His forgiveness. When we confess our sins, it causes our eyes to have their blinders taken off. We now are in a position to see the needs of those around us and we cry out in INTERCESSION for their provision, healing, deliverance, or whatever else might be their need. Then and only then, do we see our own necessity and the love that God has toward us to meet those needs. We then ASK Him for ourselves.

There is an addition aspect of Prayer that we very seldom entered into. This is when we enter into spiritual work. God, Himself has something He wants to accomplish and He asks for our COOPERATION to get it done. This kind of Prayer goes way beyond what we normally consider Prayer; it demands that we YIELD our spirit to the Holy Spirit to bring about His will. This is Cooperative Prayer.

There are elements of Intercession in this kind of Praying, such as having a Burden and Travailing. Nevertheless, here is the difference; in intercession, our concern is for the needs of others, in Cooperative Prayer, we are concerned with the desires of our God and King.

In Cooperative Prayer, we are not praying to God but Praying with God. It is our spirit alone that is involved and not our mind. Paul realizes this when He said in Rom 8:26, *"And in like manner the Spirit joins also its help to our weakness; for we do not know what we should pray for as is fitting, but the Spirit itself makes intercession with groanings which cannot be uttered. But he who searches the hearts knows what [is] the mind of the Spirit, because he intercedes for saints according to God."* Darby

Paul links this deeper Prayer life with the speaking in other tongues. On the Day of Pentecost when the Holy Spirit came upon them, they witnessed tongues resembling fire settling upon each of them and they began to speak in a different language as the Spirit gave them utterance. They came to a place that when the Holy Spirit came, they yielded to Him. Sometimes it takes waiting upon the Lord until we get to that place of yieldedness.

God is still looking for people who will yield to the Holy Spirit to bring about change. When we enter into Cooperative Prayer, we are working with God. The Holy Spirit is using our spirit and His Power is released into the physical realm.

Illustration of the HAND to show various aspects of Prayer

Thumb	Giving Thanks
Index finger	Praise
Middle finger	Confession
Ring finger	Intercession
Little finger	Asking
Palm	Cooperation

When we consider the Ministry of Prayer, we must always be conscience that we are standing before the one who is in authority. Meeting the needs for others is serious business and demands that we have the right attitude. To pray for others is more then asking, ABBA Father for an ice cream cone. To intercede for others or even when we bring a somber need of our own, is to make a petition. To bring forth a petition is to make an oral or written request, appeal or demand for a specific action. This is a governmental term and we need to take it seriously as such.

It is so important that we are mindful of - to whom we are making the petition. We are making our petition before the King of kings and the Lord of lords. There is no higher authority. There is no king that is more just, honorable, and more faithful to His

Word than He is. Everything He does is good because He is righteous and full of love for His people.

It is important for us to realize that we are citizens of His Kingdom and that is why we can come before Him with faith and assurance and make our needs known. As King, He makes a ruling regarding our petition(s) based on His Word, our faith in Him as King, and His own benevolence, love and faithfulness to His Word. His is ever mindful of His covenant that He has made with us and our obedience and adherence to the same covenant.

A WORD ABOUT OUR KING AND HIS KINGDOM IS PARAMOUNT TO US IN ORDER FOR US TO BELIEVE FOR AN ANSWER THAT WILL SATISFY OUR REQUEST. WE MUST **STOP** COMPARING GOD TO A RICH MAN THAT JUST REACHES INTO HIS POCKETS EVERY TIME WE BRING A REQUEST OR A MAJICIAN THAT REACHES INTO A HAT AND PULLS OUT A BUNNY. WE MUST **STOP** REASONING THAT GOD DOES EVERYTHING JUST BECAUSE HE IS RIGHTEOUS, GOOD AND IS FULL OF LOVE FOR HIS PEOPLE. WE MUST **STOP** THINKING THAT GOD IS OBLIGATED JUST BECAUSE WE ARE FAMILY.

GOD BRINGS JUSTICE TO OUR REQUEST BECAUSE HE IS KING AND HIS DECISIONS ARE BASED UPON THE LEGALITY OF OUR PETITION THAT HAS COME BEFORE HIS THRONE. HIS DECISION IS A GOVERNMENTAL PRONOUNCEMENT THAT YOUR PETITION HAS KINGDOM MERIT AND YOUR FAITH IN HIM IS RECOGNIZED.

His ruling is based on fairness, grace, compassion and your faith in His Word and His desire to give to you the blessings of the Kingdom. His ruling has nothing to do with our age, goodness, kindness, education or church attendance. It is based on your knowledge of the Word and faith in His authority, power and ability to follow through on His ruling.

There is one other aspect of His ruling that we need to consider; that is His ability satisfy the request. Our King has dominion over a vast kingdom and His supply is not confined to the Earth or the things of the earth. His Kingdom is a spiritual kingdom with complete access to the things of earth as well as Heaven. His resources are limitless therefore, not one of His citizens has to go without. There is not one legitimate request that will go unanswered, whether it is for forgiveness, healing, deliverance, provision or the need for love, peace or joy.

Let us look at the activity of prayer. We are prone to just start out and do what we think is best. However, even Jesus himself did not do anything without Prayer first. He prayed first: when He named His twelve disciples, before the transfiguration, He prayed before going to the Cross, in the Garden of Gethsemane. He continually admonished his disciples to pray, and He taught us even to pray for our enemies.

Why pray? So that we might reach into the spiritual realm and receive what is needed in the natural. It is Prayer that releases it or maybe better said, prayer unlocks and opens the door so that what is needed might be released to come into the natural realm.

Jesus is God but He is also man and therefore has restricted or confined Himself to the same limitations as man. Jesus prayed because He was also man and as a man, Jesus was confined to use the same keys to open the door as we have available to us.

Know the Word

The Bible has something to say about everything. It might not spell it out specifically but with the help of the Holy Spirit we can know the mind of the Lord on every subject, whether in general or specific.

We offer prayer and expect answers just because we know that God is a kind, merciful and good God. We expect answers because the person we are praying for is a good person, deserving in our eyes. We expect answers because others are hurting and we want them delivered from their pain; whether it is sickness, financial or relationship related. We ask and expect answers just because we want it so badly. We even clothe it in a desire for God to receive Glory.

It is a sad fact that 85% of the time we are disappointed because we have not considered one thing - God's Will and asking in Faith. We think we know but we have never searched it through in the Word of God. We believe that if we confess it, it will surely happen. We then wonder why so many people become disillusioned and leave the Faith. Could it possibly be because we have given them false hope and when that false hope does not materialize - out the door they go? It could be that it is not because we are asking for something that is not God's will, but that REAL faith has not sprung up in our spirit in order for it to be brought forth into life.

It is our job as Overcomers is to find out exactly what the Will of the Lord is and then pray accordingly. There are no short cuts. We cannot presume to know, we cannot wish to know, we cannot take a cursory look at Scriptures and say, "this is what is says". We must dig it out so that we know that we know what the Will of the Lord is. We cannot just have it passed down to us and accept it as truth. God's Will must be revealed to us by the Holy Spirit. We must be able to say with absolute confidence, "Thus says the Lord."

Scripture: Healing balm for the troubled

If not knowing the Will of the Lord is the biggest reason for unanswered prayer then possibly the second biggest reason is not applying Scripture in our prayer. We really do not know what the real problem is so we apply the wrong Scripture. We diagnose the symptoms as the problem. We use our natural senses to determine how we should pray and solve the problem. We need to wait upon the Holy Spirit that he might reveal to us the real problem.

We want to rush in without waiting upon the Lord. The Lord said that He would send the Holy Spirit who would lead us into all truth. Let us wait then. However, do we wait?

Paul admonishes us to pray in the Spirit. Paul says, *"I will pray with the spirit, and I will also pray with the understanding. I will sing with the spirit, and I will also sing with the understanding." 1 Cor 14:15*

Waiting can take the form of Praise, Thanksgiving, or Singing but whatever the form, we must wait until we hear from God. Many will say that I will pray with my understanding; however, this may just be because they cannot pray in tongues. From personal experience and from that of others, praying in tongues while waiting upon God frees the mind to receive revelation, whether by visions, impressions or imagery.

Guaranteed Success

Jesus had limited Himself to being a man, so he knew that if he was going to influence this world with the power of God, it was through prayer. Jesus knew something else and we must know it as well. When Jesus prayed, He knew that His prayer would be answered. If we know that our prayers are going to be answered, we too will be guaranteed success. Jesus said to His Father, *"Not my will but your will be done"* therefore He asked according to His father's will.

"Most assuredly, I say to you, he who believes in Me, the works that I do he will do also; and greater works than these he will do, because I go to My Father. And whatever you ask in My name, that I will do, that the Father may be glorified in the Son. If you ask anything in My name, I will do it. John 14:12-14

Everyone prays, atheist or not. When we are absolutely in a difficult situation with NO ONE else to turn to, we turn to some supernatural source for relief. God Almighty has made our soul to cry out when we are in deep trouble. We can take our cue from Jonah.

Then the mariners were afraid; and every man cried out to his god, and threw the cargo that was in the ship into the sea, to lighten the load. Jonah 1:5

Charles Spurgeon said so aptly, "As birds to their nest and as deer to their hiding places, so men in agony fly to a superior being for help in the hour of need".

Man in the recesses of his heart, even though he is a dethroned monarch, knows that strength is found in a supernatural being. Therefore, men are inclined to pray because of the blessing to be received.

Jesus prayed and He commands us to pray. Why pray? Because God answers prayer! He does not give us an example and tell us to do something that without an answer would amount to nothing more than just whistling in the wind. If God does not answer prayer, then you and I are fools to pray and so was Jesus.

"If it be thy will!" – Many have argued that God is sovereign or that He does not always reveal His will to us, therefore we must pray this way. They site the incident when Jesus was in the Garden just before they came to take Him to be crucified. The problem with this is, Jesus knew what was ahead of him and had no difficulty in following through with His mission. He did not have a crisis with obedience. However, He was a man without sin and the thought of becoming sin and therefore experiencing separation from His Father, was horrifying to Him. He asks His Father, if there is another way; let this cup pass from me. The Message Bible says it this way, *"Going a little ahead, he fell on his face, praying, "My Father, if there is any way, get me out of this. But please, not what I want. You do what you want."*

The Apostle John wrote in his first letter, *"If we ask anything in accordance with His will, He hears us. And if He hears us then we know that we will have the petitions that we ask of Him." John 5:14-15.* The question is not, does God desire to reveal His will to us, but rather it is; are we motivated to seek His Will?

Confidence is in the Promise. Jesus, the Savior, the Lord of lords and King of kings said, *"So I say to you, ask, and it will be given to you; seek, and you will find; knock, and it will be opened to you. For everyone who asks receives, and he who seeks finds, and to him who knocks it will be opened. Luke 11:9*

Jesus gave us absolute assurance that His Father answers Prayer when He said, "So *I say to you.*" Everything Jesus said was truth and we can believe all that He said. He created all things for His purposes and stands behind His Word. He will fulfill His word because He cannot lie.

"STIR UP THE GIFT WITHIN YOU"

Let us look more closely at another aspect of prayer that leads to effective ministry- Cooperative Prayer. Much has been written about the Gifts of the Spirit. Again, as with Faith, we have done everything to come to an understanding of the Gifts. However, understanding does not come with our mind but by our spirit. Nevertheless, we will try to bring about a clear perception of stirring up and the use of The Gifts of the Spirit.

The biggest misconception is that the Gifts are arbitrarily put into used by God with no part played by the saint. Let's us remember that God doesn't force His way on anyone. He is looking for us to cooperate with Him in ministering to others and bringing about His will.

As we try to give an understanding regarding the Gifts of the Spirit keep in mind that:

- All truths are parallel (spiritual truth is found in the physical realm revealing the truths of the spiritual)

- God really does make His way easy to understand.

If a homeowner wants a swimming pool built in his back yard, he hires a contractor. He gives him all the information needed such as size, location, depth, design, color, etc. The Contractor in turns talks to his construction superintendent, who then makes sure his has all the material and qualified personnel to do the job.

The qualified personnel is the subject under discussion. There are several different people needed to construct the pool: Backhoe operators, surveyors, concrete workers, painters, plumbers, etc. Each uses different tools to get their job completed. A plumber does not need a backhoe nor does he need to know how to operate it. Remember, it is the superintendent who knows best what tool is needed and when it is needed.

It is the same in the spiritual realm. The Gifts of the Spirit are like tools. There are nine supernatural Gifts that the Holy Spirit has at His disposal to use in order to do what Christ Jesus wants done or to solve a problem. He knows what tool is needed and when it is needed. If healing is required, a Message in Tongues or Interpretation of Tongues will not get the job done. It would be the wrong tool.

Here is something that my pastor, Clarence E. Fast did for me 38 years ago. Our church regularly had an alter service, with many coming from a variety of denominations. One Sunday night, Dr. Fast called me forward and said, "I want you to help me tonight praying for the people. However, do not ask them the reason why they are coming forward, permit only the Holy Spirit to tell you what to do. As He reveals it to you, though whatever means (direct word, vision, impression or imagery), speak exactly as He tells you."

Knowledge of the true PROBLEM by vision, impressions or imagery is an act of the Holy Spirit. This goes way beyond sensing something. It is knowing, what God knows. The person to whom we are ministering may think he/she is the only human being that knows and that is probably true– but God knows and He then passes that information on to us.

The Holy Spirit knows what Gift is needed to meet the PROBLEM. It might be a miracle (floating an axe, turning water into wine, walking on water). It might be Faith that gets the job done even in the face of the seemingly impossible, or it might be an application of the healing that Jesus has provided in the atonement. What is needed might be deliverance from an evil spirit that has gone undetected and allowed to act freely in a person's life.

The Holy Spirit provides the right Gift at the right time when we wait on Him. We might ask, HOW DO I KNOW WHAT GIFT IS NEEDED? When the Holy Spirit reveals the PROBLEM (by the way- it is not the need but the Problem that is to be addressed) He stirs up the right gift within us.

The BIGGER Question is, how do we wait on the Holy Spirit in order to receive the revelation? Praying in the spirit is the answer. When you pray in tongues, it is your spirit that is praying. As you continue praying, you go from one level to another in prayer. It is then that you are entering into Cooperative Prayer.

When you begin to speak in your native language, you speak forth from your spirit what the Holy Spirit has revealed to you. It may make no sense to you at all. But the person you are speaking to, will know exactly what is meant. You might then call forth from the spiritual realm and speak it into the physical realm.

If we are to win the battles against Satan and his demons, if we are to win the hearts of men so that they may follow Jesus, we must do more than believe in the Gifts of the Spirit. There must be more than an acceptance of words in a Statement of Faith. There must be a release of those Gifts from within in order to defeat the enemy.

In the same way that the Son of God was manifested for the purpose of making visible, the invisible God, that He might destroy the works of the devil; Spiritual Gifts are given to manifest, or to make visible, the invisible God and His awesome power through us.

The people that have been entrusted to our care are in need. They have turned to us because we have offered them the promise of hope. The Gifts of the Spirit give evidence that God is at work. It is not us; it is God working through His Church. He is revealing, not only His power, but His love, grace, and mercy through us. Will we disappoint them?

It must become personal. Our spirit must become involved if we are to minister effectively. The Holy Spirit desires to flow through our spirit, not our mind. Jesus was touched by our infirmities. He was moved by our need. If prayer is only mechanical, then we will be just as surprised at the results as the one for whom we are praying.

Jesus was moved with compassion. In other words, He was moved to do something. He was moved to provide the answer to the need. His spirit cried out for that answer.

In those days, the multitude being very great and having nothing to eat, Jesus called His disciples to Him and said to them, "I have compassion on the multitude, because they have now continued with Me three days and have nothing to eat. And if I send them away hungry to their own houses, they will faint on the way; for some of them have come from afar." Mark 8:1-3

There are many more examples in Scripture to illustrate this point. We must feel their pain (bear one another burdens) as well as being involved mentally if we are to minister effectively.

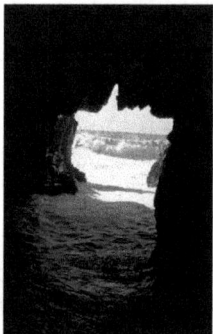

THE LINK BETWEEN PRAYER AND FAITH: "THE CALLING FORTH"

Throughout the Bible, God calls to the unseen and calls things to come into the seen. He calls to that which is not, as if it were.

Picture this: A man in a cave, hidden way back in the recesses of the darkness. He is involved in doing his own thing. He is making the best of his situation. Deep down, however, he really wants to get out. If he does not want to get out it is because he is hiding and does not want to face the consequences of his actions.

What if someone calls out to him; actually calls him by name. Just the mention of his name draws his attention. There is something about being "called" that is so different from being commanded. As he responds and draws closer to the one doing the calling, he is actually getting closer and closer to the light. This light is like nothing he has ever seen before. His first thought is to react because it is so different from the darkness that he is accustomed to and has found comfort in. But as he allows himself to get used to this light he begins to *respond* instead of *react* as before. As he responds to the light, he eventually steps into the light and he is finally free from the cave and the darkness that held him captive.

God calls us to come out from the darkness into His marvelous light. God calls the dead to come back to life. He calls for the waters of the sea to be poured out. He calls for unbelievers to come out from captivity.

In as much as we are to be Christ's Ambassadors, we are to use His authority in such a way that it will bring Glory to His name. We are to use the Name of Jesus in commanding demons or evil spirits to come out of those in bondage. We are to commanded sicknesses to leave.

What we are dealing with is the spiritual realm. We have been so accustomed to thinking and dwelling on the natural realm that we get confused and ignore the real possibilities that are available to us in the spiritual realm.

Illustration: I had one son who was a builder and another who is in construction. I have another son that is a budding artist and three grandchildren that love to draw and actually are very good. Here is the point! All of these people think beyond the one dimension. They go beyond the second dimension to the third dimension: the 3-D.

If we are to move in the faith realm when we pray, we must go still higher. We must go higher in order to get a Mountain View perspective as we mentioned in Chapter Three of our first book. If we continue to look up instead of looking down, we will never see what God sees. We will never receive the vision that can become reality.

FOUR DIMENSIONS OF SEEING

One dimension –The Line

Two dimensional – The Plane

Three dimensional - The Cube

The first three above belong to the earth; they are in the realm of the natural. We want to go higher, higher into the realm of the supernatural. It is there in this higher dimension, the fourth dimension that we must reach for and be involved.

Fourth dimension - The Spirit

When we live in this new realm, we are living with the **Realizing Power.** This is the life of Christ being lived out through us. Paul wrote about this life when he said in Col 1:27

"To them God willed to make known what are the riches of the glory of this mystery among the Gentiles: which is Christ in you, the hope of glory".

Paul writes of Abraham:

"Therefore it is of faith that it might be according to grace, so that the promise might be sure to all the seed, not only to those who are of the law, but also to those who are of the faith of Abraham. Abraham, who is the father of us all (as it is written, "I have made you a father of many nations") in the presence of Him whom he believed — God, who gives life to the dead and calls those things which do not exist as though they did". Rom 4:16-17

Here we have God calling those things, which do not exist as though they did. WOW, imagine that, calling things that do not exist as though as did. Even Abram starts to call himself-Abraham (Father of a nation) before Sarah is pregnant.

Let us look at the way Jesus exercised his faith in this truth:

- He calls to the unseen to come into the seen

- He calls those in darkness to come into the light

- He calls those dead back to life

- He calls those that are lost to be found

- He calls bodies that are sick to be healed.

- He calls the possessed to be of sound mind and commands demons to come out

Here then is the Link. This, Fourth dimension living, is the life to which our King has called us. In the previous topic regarding Prayer, we noted that we must believe that we will have success when we ask God for something. Here is where most people stop. They want to leave everything up to God. It is the same way when people ask us for something. They want, without cost. However, we are living in the same realm as God, therefore, he expects us to act in the same way as He.

This is where Cooperative Prayer comes in. When we enter into Cooperative Prayer, our spirit unites itself with the Holy Spirit. Just as the Holy Spirit hovered over the Earth, waiting for the Word to be spoken so He could go to work, He is waiting for us to speak that which God wants to do in this realm so He can go to work.

God wants us to be involved. Therefore, He has given us examples throughout the Bible that we can follow. He Himself began Creation and while the Spirit was brooding, hovering over the face of the earth, He said, "Let there be light". He called "light" to appear when there was no light. He called "those things which be not as though they were". God writes of Abraham who followed His example and did the same thing. See Roman 4:17 above. Therefore, we are to do the same.

Putting Faith and Prayer together:

As we mentioned in our discussion on Faith, Faith is the substance of things hoped for. "Hoped for"; that is the key. What is it that you are hoping? Are you just looking for a car, a job, a house, a husband or wife? If that is the case then you will probably take whatever comes your way, whether you really like it or not. In our treatment on Vision, we said that a vision must be a clear-cut image from God. The same is true here. How will you ever know it is God, who has answered your prayer, if you just asked in generalities? You must be specific, more detailed. You must have a Vision of that which you are praying for and calling out.

The Lord grants the desires of your heart, when you delight in Him. This cannot be just a want or a wish; this must be a passion. It must be something, that without, you cannot live. You must have it for the Lord's work or to fulfill the plan He has for your life. It is a burning passion within you. If there is just such a passion within you, you will never have peace until you know that you know that this passion will be satisfied. You must possess a Passion to receive the Vision for which you are praying.

Are there tears on your pillow from crying out to the Lord for that which you are praying? If so, there is only one thing you can do; seek the Lord, pray until you receive His assurance. Sadly, here is where most STOP, even the faithful. They ask, they cry out, they call out, but they cannot find the time to wait upon the Lord. Years ago, we called this "Praying Through".

Unfortunately, most Christians today know nothing of tarrying before the Lord and getting this breakthrough in their faith. The benefits are REAL. When you wait upon the Lord until you have the assurance that your passion will be satisfied, then you will know, that you know, that you know, that you will receive the object of your hope. We must seek the Lord for Assurance.

There are laws in the spiritual realm and to receive the benefits you must abide by them. Jesus said, *"according to your faith be it unto you"*. James said, *"you have faith and I have works: show me your faith without your works, and I will show you my faith by my works"*. What they were saying in modern language is, "Where's the beef?" In other words, where is the evidence of your faith?

96

It very well may be in your physical works or it may be in your words. In reality, it will be in your speech first. You may say it to yourself, to your wife, to your best friend, or maybe to God as a matter of giving thanks. Nevertheless, you are speaking it forth. You must Speak the word which has been put in your heart.

Prayer is not just asking; it is a means of warfare

The Bible says that we all have been given a measure of faith. It is through this faith (our faith) that God brings about His "good works".

- *how God anointed Jesus of Nazareth with the Holy Spirit and with power, who went about **doing good** and healing all who were oppressed by the devil, for God was with Him Acts 10:38.*

- *Eternal life to those who by patient continuance in **doing good** seek for glory, honor, and immortality; Rom 2:7*

- *And let us not grow weary while **doing good**, for in due season we shall reap if we do not lose heart. Gal 6:9*

- *But as for you, brethren, do not grow weary in **doing good**. 2 Thessalonians 3:13*

- *For this is the will of God, that by **doing good** you may put to silence the ignorance of foolish men 1 Peter 2:15*

- *For it is better, if it is the will of God, to suffer for **doing good** than for doing evil. 1 Peter 3:17*

- *Therefore let those who suffer according to the will of God commit their souls to Him in **doing good**, as to a faithful Creator. 1 Peter 4:19*

I submit that prayer does not mean giving God our to-do list and watch Him do it, while we hide our lights underneath the bushes. When we pray God wants to do more than do the work for us. He answers us with wisdom and sends us forth with Kingdom assignments to represent Him in this world – when the righteous are in authority the city rejoices. Yes, believers need to act, get involved and NOT withdraw themselves from culture or politics.

Jesus, in doing good, went about healing the sick, raising the dead. He gave peace to the troubled, confidence to those with fear, mercy and forgiveness to those caught in sin. He had compassion on the suffering and brought deliverance to those possessed by demons. He calls upon us to do the same. The Gospel of the Kingdom is a dynamic Gospel. He wants to bear the burdens of the hopeless and bring victory to the suffering, therefore in our "doing good", it means being in conflict with our enemy.

Jesus said to those that believe: *"Go into all the world and preach the gospel to every creature. He who believes and is baptized will be saved; but he who does not believe will be condemned. And these signs will follow those who believe: In My name they will cast out demons; they will speak with new tongues; they will take up serpents; and if they drink anything deadly, it will by no means hurt them; they will lay hands on the sick, ad they will recover."* Mark 16:15-18

WARRIOR FOR CHRIST

From our discussion on Worldview conflicts, we have seen that a real problem Overcomers are facing is that of deception. We find ourselves face to face against Humanism, secularism, a scientific worldview, and a mixture of alternative supernatural groups saying the same as us, "This is the way".

Paul warned Timothy and us about this very day, *"But know this, that in the last days perilous times will come: For men will be lovers of themselves, lovers of money, boasters, proud, blasphemers, disobedient to parents, unthankful, unholy, unloving, unforgiving, slanderers, without self-control, brutal, despisers of good, traitors, headstrong, haughty, lovers of pleasure rather than lovers of God, having a form of godliness but denying its power. And from such people turn away".* 2 Tim 3:1-6

As we pointed out in the last topic on prayer, many of us want to step out of our comfort zone and be used by God to touch others for an eternity. Nevertheless, in order to do so, we need to do more than just move from simply understanding the Principles of truth, to walking in its power.

A Time to Confront

This is the time to confront the enemy. The Holy Spirit is calling God's people to prayer and praise but is also equipping them for Spiritual Warfare and the coming harvest.

When we proclaim Christ and his Kingdom to others and release the Gifts of the Spirit, we are manifesting the supernatural presence of an unseen God. We are confronting Satan and his demons head on. The conflict between Worldviews is on and God is winning.

As we witness the events being played out in the world, we need to realize that it is not what is seen that we need to be concerned about but the unseen. We are witnessing the confrontation of two kingdoms. The one ruled by Satan and the other ruled by Jesus. One kingdom is invading another. Satan is on the defensive, although knowing that he has already lost. Jesus is on the offensive and has given His Church (the called out ones) the authority, the armor, and the weapons necessary to wage war and win.

Paul gives us the picture of these two kingdoms in Colossians 1:13, *"He has delivered us from the power of darkness and conveyed us into the kingdom of the Son of His love."* The first is a kingdom of slavery and the second is a kingdom of freedom. To us that are maturing citizens of His kingdom, Jesus bestows upon us an anointing. This anointing is for conflict. This anointing is for us to set the captives free by attacking those that would enslave the peoples of the world and keep them in darkness.

Jesus is invading the world we live in and He has brought His Kingdom's authority with Him. We saw from Luke 10:9 that the seventy were to heal the sick and say to those that would listen, *"The Kingdom has come near to you".* Our authority comes from this kingdom. It is kingdom authority. We are not to use our own authority (human- even great as it might be) because it comes not from our position, but this authority comes from a relationship to the King.

The Apostle Paul writes in Eph 6:10-13, *"Finally, my brethren, be strong in the Lord and in the power of His might. Put on the whole armor of God that you may be able to stand against the wiles of the devil; For we do not wrestle against flesh and blood, but against principalities, against powers, against the rulers of the darkness of this age, against spiritual hosts of wickedness in the heavenly places. Therefore take up the whole armor of God, that you may be able to withstand in the evil day, and having done all, to stand."*

Again, he writes in 2 Cor. 10:3-6, *"For though we walk in the flesh, we do not war according to the flesh. For the weapons of our warfare are not carnal but mighty in God for pulling down strongholds, casting down arguments and every high thing that exalts itself against the knowledge of God, bringing every thought into captivity to the obedience of Christ, and being ready to punish all disobedience when your obedience is fulfilled".*

Christians bring into their new relationship with God, baggage just as men and women do when they enter marriage. Because Satan and his demons have been chasing and tormenting us for years we must now chase him and take back that which he has stolen from us and from God as well. As Overcomers, we must bring Deliverance from the effects of carrying that baggage to others where Satan has been allowed to establish his control.

Spiritual Warfare is not just in the Mind. Satan and his followers attach every area of life's existence. We find him attacking our families, our finances, our health, our sexuality, our relationships, our contracts, and our worship, plus more. We must take our warfare to the streets and be on the offensive in order that the Kingdom of God can be re-established in others.

Jesus demonstrated how we are to set the "Captive Free" when He healed the sick and used His authority to cast out demons. Throughout my experience and that of many others, this setting free and staying free has been to those who profess a faith in Jesus Christ as King of Kings. Those that have no desire to take up their cross and follow Jesus almost 100% of the time, NEVER are delivered or go back into bondage once they are alone and tempted again. Those that desire to be set free must be willing to "expose open doors", "close those doors", "go through Deliverance" and "do those things that enables them to stay free".

We must fully understand that every committed Believer has the authority to combat satanic deception. We have the Holy Spirit within and when Baptized in The Holy Spirit, we are equipped with power to invade Satan's kingdom, pull down strongholds and expel evil spirits that have people in bondage.

Chapter 6
Ministry in Action

THE CHURCH'S CALL TO ACTION

All during the first two centuries, the Saints, as well as the five-fold ministry, were involved in ministry. They were ministering outside the walls of the church building to their friends and neighbors. However, in the years following the 3rd Century, the task of serving the saints and winning the lost became the occupation of the professional clergy. The Church, *by allowing a few to minister to the many*, promoted Satan's most effective strategy to stop the spread of the Gospel of the Kingdom throughout the world.

Before Jesus left this Earth, He set in place a plan enabling His Disciples to receive instruction that would establish them in their faith. He set in place Apostles, Prophets, Evangelists, Pastors and Teachers and charged them with the responsibility to mature the saints so they could take the message of the Kingdom to the whole world. Nevertheless, beginning with the 3rd Century, the Church initiated its own plan that took the work of the Lord out of the hands of the disciples and placed it in the hands of the Clergy.

Satan knows that it is in serving that the Holy Spirit brings about the Transformation whereby the image of Christ is formed in us. Therefore, he uses every tactic to prevent God's people from doing acts of *service* and being fruitful in ministry. For those that have the responsibility of equipping the Saints to "Catch the Wind", the warfare increases.

Since our presupposition is that God's Grand Plan for Believers is to rule and reign with Christ, then the Believers must be prepared to do so. Paul writes in Rom 8:14-15, *"For as many as are led by the Spirit of God, these are sons of God."* It is the sons that will rule and reign with Christ, not just because we are Believers.

To rule and reign is ministry – *service* to others. Therefore, we must have experience *serving* before being promoted. The ministry of the twelve, the seventy, the seven Deacons, the Apostles and Prophets were all men who had proven their faithful service first before being promoted. They were men of good reputation, full of the Holy Spirit and wisdom. These were men of faith and power and with love for others.

It is in *service* that our faith, hope and love are truly tested. It is in *service* that others see what we are really "made of". It is in *service* that we have an opportunity to mature and develop our relationship with the Holy Spirit and learn to be led by Him.

Throughout *BORN TO RULE*, we presented the picture of a Disciple who has become Kingdom-centered as opposed to man-centered. I know we all want to present Christ as the answer to all of our needs, but this is only half the story. God does desire to meet our deepest needs but in reality, many of our needs are met as we give ourselves in service to Jesus Christ and to others.

The Bible tells us that those who are willing to lose their lives will find them. It is in giving that we find true fulfillment. Luke 6:38 says it best, *"Give and it will be given to you: good measure, pressed down, shaken together, and running over will be put into your bosom. For with the same measure that you use, it will be measured back to you".* It is not just referring to money but our whole being.

Ministry is bringing the supernatural power of God to those in need. The Bible pictures the Church as the body of Christ therefore, as a body; each member has a part in its activity. The hand cannot say it has no need of the foot or the eye that it has no need of the ear. The parts of the body are joined together to

104

function in unity. Each Believer has something to offer to the rest of the body.

When we speak of ministry, we are referring to bringing the spiritual into the natural realm. It is important that you work together with someone of like faith so that you might affect change in the lives of people, our cities and our nation. We must agree together, present a united front against the enemy, and show people that God loves them. There are several facets of ministry; following are some of them.

INTERCESSION

Intercession – It is the technical term for approaching a King. We are seeking an audience with the King on the behalf of others. Intercession has "intent". There is a purpose for our activity. Our mind is involved as there is a goal that is to be attained. It has reference to a specific outcome. Our spirit is also involved as this "intent" consumes our being. We are passionate for the intended outcome.

Throughout this book, we have stressed the ongoing and growing relationship between our Father and us. We have stressed the oneness that must be developed with the King and ourselves. We have stressed our obedience and submission to the Holy Spirit. It is our total involvement with God that we bring into Intercession.

Intercession engulfs our totally being and causes our pillows to be wet with tears. Intercession is a result of Passion. Intercession involves our spirit, soul and our body.

One of the best examples of intercession is found in Gen 18, when Abraham speaks to God on behalf of Sodom. His plea is full of compassion as he is concerned with the well-being of others rather than his own needs. Such selfless concern is the true mark of all intercessory prayers. He has alive within him, the Cross Principle as discussed earlier in BORN TO RULE.

When we discussed Prayer, we considered that which must be birthed within in order to be effective in ministry. However, there are additional considerations we must take into account when we enter into Intercession.

"baros" Greek for "burden" – *"Bear one another's burdens, and so fulfill the law of Christ."* Gal 6:2-3. A burden makes a demand on your resources and has reference to weight – Heavy. It presses upon you and persists until it is lifted. A burden will come before a breakthrough. It comes before the enemy has completed his work. Satan attacks but before he can claim victory, we intercede.

The burden that comes from the Holy Spirit comes suddenly and needs immediate attention. He gives energy and you will receive no peace or release until you pray through and the answer is forth coming. However, as suddenly as the burden has come, if you do not respond, it will leave. When it leaves, because of disobedience, it will most likely never return and you will have missed your chance to make a difference in your world.

A burden comes like an overshadowing as it did to Mary, Jesus' mother. Our spirit becomes like as a womb carrying the life that God has put there by the Holy Spirit.

To bear one another's burden is to say, "Your pain is my pain". Through identification, we may be the channel as well as a willing participant in the answer, *"Then Jesus said, "Father, forgive them, for they do not know what they do." Luke 23:34*

"yalad" Greek for "travail" - *"My little children, for whom I labor in birth again until Christ is formed in you" Gal 4:19-20.* There are times when we receive a burden because God wants our involvement in the fulfillment of His plan. Travail is the act of bringing the burden to birth, often characterized by weeping, groaning and pleading. It can be noisy just as a maternity ward is noisy.

We pray life into a situation as Christ did for Lazarus and it may last only for a moment as in giving birth. We must let the Holy Spirit control us and let Him do as He pleases. Just as you cannot stop in the middle of childbirth, we cannot stop halfway through intercession until the burden lifts. If you stop, it will be a stillbirth.

Travail, as in labor, starts when it is time for the process to begin and ends when the thing is born. It is as simple as that.

What is happening during this travail period? It is warfare! It is the act of working the burden through the birth canal. This is characterized by binding, loosing and demanding,

Jesus cried over Jerusalem because He knew of the impending doom that was coming, not just for the city that was going to be destroyed (temporal) but also for the nation of Israel that was like sheep without a shepherd (eternal).

We are called "a Royal Priesthood" in I Peter 2: 9. We are royalty but we are still Priests. A Priest stands as a mediator, between God and man. Jesus is King over the Earth, yet He too is a Priest; yes even our High Priest who is our advocate to the Father.

Listen to the Scriptures as they reveal our Lord and the Holy Spirit in the act of intercession:

- *And He was numbered with the transgressors, And He bore the sin of many, And made intercession for the transgressors. Isa 53:12*

- *but the Spirit Himself makes intercession for us with groanings which cannot be uttered. Rom 8:26*

- *Now He who searches the hearts knows what the mind of the Spirit is, because He makes intercession for the saints according to the will of God. Rom 8:27*

- *Who is he who condemns? It is Christ who died, and furthermore is also risen, who is even at the right hand of God, who also makes intercession for us. Rom 8:34*

- *Therefore, He is also able to save to the uttermost those who come to God through Him, since He always lives to make intercession for them. Heb 7:25*

Listen to the cry of our Lord in what we refer to as The Lord's prayer. This is fervent effectual prayer. This kind of prayer moves mountains.

EXPANDING OUR INFLUENCE

There is one aspect of intercession that we must mention again, making sure we completely understand. We must have a Kingdom mentality. Intercession involves more than self, family and our church. We, the Church, must begin thinking in terms of getting out of our box and not restricting our prayers to just those around us.

"basilia" Greek for "royal power, dominion" –Luke uses this word when he mentions the Kingdom in Luke 17:20-21. *"Now when He was asked by the Pharisees when the kingdom of God would come, He answered them and said, "The kingdom of God does not come with observation; nor will they say, 'See here!' or 'See there!' For indeed, the kingdom of God is within you." Luke 17:20-21*

Therefore, it is our mission to establish His Kingdom throughout the world - through prayer. Jesus said, *"And from the days of John the Baptist until now, the kingdom of heaven suffers violence, and the violent take it by force. "Matt 11:12-13*

The Kingdom of God is a spiritual kingdom where the right or authority to rule over a kingdom is exercised. The right to use this authority is conferred on us who are "Born Again"; to use on His behalf.

Through intercession, we can go around the world without stepping one foot outside our door. The Kingdom of God is at hand when His rule is acknowledged. God has not relinquished His sovereignty in the face of rebellion, demoniac or human, but has declared His purpose to establish it. It is the mission of the Church to intercede for our communities, state, country and even the whole world.

Here is an example. Four months ago, my good friend, Dub Lewis from Acts Ministries Today, was ministering in the middle of Africa. Dub seeks out those who have never heard the name of Jesus and ministers to them with demonstration of the power of the Holy Spirit.

It was his last day in that area and he was speaking to a group of witch doctors regarding the Kingdom. I was in Florida and praying as I do while completing my daily walk. I had been praying for about 15 minutes when all of a sudden a burden came over me to pray for Dub. I started praying in tongues and immediately my prayer language changed to something I had never experienced before. I began praying in an African dialect and with an emotional intensity that I immediately knew that I was no longer praying for Dub, I was interceding for Dub on God's behalf.

This went on for about 10 minutes and just as suddenly as it came, it left and my prayer language returned to normal. When Dub returned home, I called him and he told me what had happened. He was talking with several witch doctors and the spiritual fate of the whole village was at stake. If the Holy Spirit did not penetrate their hearts, he would not be able to come back and share the Gospel of the Kingdom. - HE WILL BE GOING BACK.

EVANGELISM

The Good News that Jesus gave to the Jewish people was the Gospel of the Kingdom. Throughout the Gospels, we read of Jesus telling His Disciples about the Kingdom. For forty days after Jesus rose from the dead, He spoke to His Disciples about the Kingdom. Peter and Paul spoke about the Gospel of the Kingdom as well as did other Apostles and Disciples.

We stated that Part One of Our Mission is – "Restore man to Fellowship with his Creator." Therein we told of the need to love and give acceptance to those we want to reach. They need to know that we accept them for who they are and wherever they are in life. They need to feel that our love for them is real. This is our starting point. They must see that we are ready and willing to sacrifice what we have for their wellbeing.

They must know that we believe what we are telling them is the truth, with no hesitation and no doubt whatsoever. They must know that we are not ashamed of the Gospel of the Kingdom. We must know that our gospel is the power of God unto salvation.

Paul tells us why he was so effective in ministry, *"Brethren, my heart's desire and prayer to God for Israel is that they may be saved. For I bear them witness that they have a zeal for God, but not according to knowledge. For they being ignorant of God's righteousness, and seeking to establish their own righteousness, have not submitted to the righteousness of God; For Christ is the end of the law for righteousness to everyone who believes"*. *Romans 10:1-4* Paul knew what he believed.

Paul goes on to say in *Romans 10:14-15, "How then shall they call on Him in whom they have not believed? And how shall they believe in Him of whom they have not heard? And how shall they hear without a preacher? And how shall they preach unless they are sent? As it is written: "How beautiful are the feet of those who preach the gospel of peace, who bring glad tidings of good things!"*

Paul isn't just talking here of the paid clergy, he is talking here of all Believers. We are all to preach the Good News of the Kingdom and of Jesus Christ.

This is what we need to look for when we are sharing the Gospel. There are **four** words beginning with "C", occurring in the following order.

- **Conviction of Sin** – Conviction starts with awareness that a Holy God has laws that govern His kingdom. These laws cannot be disobeyed without consequence.

- **Contriteness of Heart** – This is awareness that we are guilty as charged as we stand in front of a Holy God that demands justice.

- **Confession of Sin** –A sincere sorrow for what we have done and an awareness of God's forgiveness brings us to repentance. This is personal.

- **Conversion of the Soul** – Faith that God will redeem us and make us new creature in Christ, brings about an awareness of NEW LIFE.

Sharing the Gospel is like fishing, so let us go fishing:

Fishing Hole - We must ask The Father, who knows the hearts of all men, where to find hungry fish.

Timing - As we look at people and see their body language, we need to sense their hunger and willingness to eat of what we have to say. Find out what is causing their hunger.

Bait - Citizenship in the Kingdom (Eternity and Now). The bait needs to be big enough and meaningful to them in order for them to listen tentatively.

Hook - God's unconditional Love must come up within us, flow out from us and they must know that God loves them unconditionally.

Line - How much do you share? Some will pay special attention while others will just listen, some will want to hear more. We need to pay attention to their attention span.

Reel - Use your testimony, be sensitive to their response, and reel them in when they are hooked.

Here is the problem; Many have already heard of Heaven and think of it as a place to go after death. Because they have not seen a need for a savior or seen proof of a real Jesus in the lives of the people who call themselves Christians, they have dismissed what the Church has preached. What they have not heard about is the Kingdom of God and therefore are not looking for a king. We have emphasized a Savior that will take us to Heaven when we die instead of a King who will provide for and protect us while we live for Him. In reality, the King came to be our Savior.

Here is the answer; Because of our faith (assurance and confidence) in the finished work of Jesus Christ, we are reconciled to the Father. The Father created all things through His Son; including setting up His Kingdom here on earth. We need to bring their attention to the Kingdom. Jesus is the only door into the Kingdom of God; there is only one Kingdom, one way into the Kingdom and only one king.

We need to talk about citizenship in a kingdom, and not escaping to Heaven. Heaven is a place but what needs to be emphasized is that it is place where God's government is set up. The Father made Jesus, King of the Earth, even though HE is in Heaven. He rules from Heaven in the hearts of His disciples. His Disciples, using His authority and the power of the Holy Spirit are to take dominion over the Earth on His behalf.

Jesus sits at the Father's right hand in Heaven waiting for the day when He will return for His bride. Then, after the marriage supper of the Lamb, He will return to Earth riding on His white horse to set up His throne in Jerusalem. He shall conquer all the thrones of man and He will rule for a thousand years. At this point we will rule and reign with Him.

LAYING ON OF HANDS

The early Church practiced the Laying on of Hands. However, in the 3rd and 4th century it began to cease. The Church was then plunged into the Dark Ages and the Laying on of Hands soon after became only a ritual.

Since the Reformation, God has been restoring truths that has been lost; the Gifts of the Holy Spirit and the Laying on of Hands, being among them. God is again using this practice to give impartation, confirmation and blessing to His people. To lay hands on someone is to touch the other and to communicate something of yourself to them through that touch.

The function of this book is to move the disciple along the road to maturity in order that he may be prepared to rule and reign with Christ and to be a blessing to others during this journey. The author of Hebrews 5 is exhorting his readers to leave behind childish things and grow into a New Man, "of full age". He says to the reader, *"Therefore, leaving the discussion of the elementary principles of Christ, let us go on to perfection, not laying again the foundation of repentance from dead works and of faith toward God, of the doctrine of baptisms, of laying on of hands, of resurrection of the dead, and of eternal judgment"*. Heb 6:1-3

These things, he says, are elementary principles. They should be commonplace. What did God have in mind when He established the Laying on of Hands?

With the hand, we take hold of and take control of things once not in our control. The hand represents POWER. The hand is stretched out with might and is strong and mighty. When a strong hand is stretched out, it brings fear into the heart of those who are opposed. When the hand holds a weapon, it brings terror to the enemy because of the destructive power it holds.

The hand is also used to bring blessing. The hands of a father laid upon his oldest son, signifies that that son receives a greater portion than the others.

We see from the following scriptures, the Laying on of Hands is used to:

Minister the following:

Healing ---- *And many hearing Him were astonished, saying," Where did this Man get these things? And what wisdom is this which is given to Him, that such mighty works are performed by His hands... Now He could do no mighty work there, except that He laid His hands on a few sick people and healed them. Mark 6:2,5*

Then they brought to Him one who was deaf and had an impediment in his speech, and they begged Him to put His hand on him. Mark 7:32

Signs and wonders ---- *And through the hands of the apostles many signs and wonders were done among the people. Acts 5:12*

The Baptism in the Holy Spirit ---- *And Ananias went his way and entered the house; and laying his hands on him he said, "Brother Saul, the Lord Jesus, who appeared to you on the road as you came, has sent me that you may receive your sight and be filled with the Holy Spirit." Acts 9:17*

To impart spiritual gifts ----- *Do not neglect the gift that is in you, which was given to you by prophecy with the laying on of the hands of the eldership. 1 Tim 4:14*

Therefore, I remind you to stir up the gift of God, which is in you through the laying on of my hands. 2 Tim 1:6-7

For I long to see you, that I may impart to you some spiritual gift, so that you may be established — Rom 1:11

Identification ----*Then he shall put his hand on the head of the burnt offering, and it will be accepted on his behalf to make atonement for him. Lev 1:4*

And he shall lay his hand on the head of his offering, and kill it at the door of the tabernacle of meeting; and Aaron's sons, the priests, shall sprinkle the blood all around on the altar. Lev 3:2

Do not lay hands on anyone hastily, nor share in other people's sins; keep yourself pure. 1 Tim 5:22

The Laying on of Hands is not to be a ritual but a dynamic means of bringing God's grace and mercy to His people. The Laying on of Hands is God's way to transfer the Power within you to those that are in need. Note: You cannot give what you do not have.

CASTING OUT DEMONS PRAYER FOR THE SICK

Satan's agents are called by various names including: demons, unclean spirits and evil spirits. The word, Devil, is a name given only to Satan. Therefore, there is only one Devil but many demons.

It is best to clear up another misconception at the beginning; a Christian may have a demon but not be possessed. To be "possessed" implies ownership. A "Born Again" Believer is bought with a price, the precious blood of Jesus. However, a Believer may be influenced or be oppressed by a demon or demons.

When a Believer receives Christ into his life, if he was sick or influenced by a demon to such an extent that the person seems to have no control (pornography, cursing), he is saved but not delivered. Therefore, in order for that Believer to be set free, the

114

demon(s) must be cast out, driven out or expelled (all these words mean the same).

I have broken down demon activity into three areas – spiritual, physical and mental or emotional; SPIRITUAL meaning a case of demon possession of the Unbeliever, PHYSICAL relating to sickness and disease and MENTAL OR EMOTIONAL relating to serious strongholds of the Devil that usually involve many demons of various strengths. It has been my experience; demons causing sickness come out more readily than demons that cause disease. Demons causing mental traumas are more difficult yet.

In apprehension of causing more harm than not, I want to caution ministers to move slowly in this area of casting out demons. Demons causing mental or emotional disturbance are more difficult to cast out. Unless one is prepared for some real spiritual battle these are best left alone until a more seasoned Believer is there with you. You might also refer to www.warfareplus.com for more information and help

The demons of infirmity attack people in their body singularly but others may join in because they have found an open door through the emotions. This would be especially true of those illnesses that are more devastating such as cancer, diabetes, MS and others.

How shall we proceed when face to face with a demon? Ministry is Spiritual. It may take place in the physical but the battle starts in the spiritual. Ministry is warfare between two kingdoms. Our King gives us permission to His name, the name of Jesus, to invoke because ALL authority is given to Him. We are His representatives and He calls upon us to set the captives free in order to finish the work that He started. This is spiritual warfare and we must engage our spirit to speak or command demons to come out of those to whom we are ministering.

Demons need physical bodies to inhabit, as that is how they fulfill their mission. Humans were not born with demon oppression but somewhere in their life, they opened the door through some activity or emotional experience. Some physical oppression results in seizures, convulsions, craziness, or affecting hearing, speech and eyesight.

Unclean spirits are often the causes of sexual oppressions.

Evil spirits affect humans in such a way was to cause or influence the person to do mean, hurtful, sinful activities that will eventually find that person in jail or in some other serious trouble.

Our purpose in ministry is not to show the person in need how much we know or how nice we can pray. It is to set them free. They do not need to know what is causing their problem, but they must have faith, that as a citizen, Jesus wants them healed. They must know that it is God's will for them to be healed. Knowing that they have citizenship in the Kingdom is the key to their faith.

Not all sicknesses or diseases are the result of demons, as I believe they are in the case for diabetes, cancer, or even the flu. The Earth is under a curse and what was created "good", now is influenced by evil and has turned against man. Mosquitoes were not created to carry germs or to bite humans but are now seen as pests and are to be killed. Therefore, as ministers, we do not always cast out demons but we do need to use our authority to bring healing to the body.

How to begin to cast out demons or sickness and disease

First - Using the authority of the King, we can speak to the demon or sickness and command (remember this is warfare) it to come out of that person. Don't look at the body; the warfare is spiritual and must be won in the spiritual realm before it is manifested in the physical realm. Sometimes the demon(s) or sickness will not come out at once, but stand your ground and command again. The demon or sickness can sense if you really know of your authority or if you are bluffing. You will know in your spirit if it has left.

THE LEVEL OF YOUR AUTHORITY RECOGNIZED BY DEMON(S) OR SICKNESS IS PROPORTIONAL TO THE LEVEL OF AUTHORITY THAT YOU SUBJECT YOURSELF. IF YOU ARE NOT COMPLETELY OBEDIENT AND

SUBMISSIVE TO YOUR KING, DON'T EXPECT THE DEMON OR SICKNESS TO BE
READILY OBEDIENT OR SUBMISSIVE TO YOU – NO MATTER HOW LOUD YOU
GET OR HOW LONG YOU COMMAND. YOU'LL JUST WEAR YOURSELF OUT AS
WELL AS THE PERSON IN NEED.

*And these signs will follow those who believe: In My name they will cast
out demons; they will speak with new tongues; they will take up serpents;
and if they drink anything deadly, it will by no means hurt them; they
will lay hands on the sick, and they will recover." Mark 16:17-18*

*Jesus said, "If I cast out demons by Beelzebub, by whom do your sons
cast them out? Therefore they will be your judges. But if I cast out
demons with the finger of God, surely the kingdom of God has come upon
you". Luke 11:19-21*

Second – After you sense the demon has left, speak healing to
the body. Jesus has already made it possible for healing to return
to the body. We are not speaking to the person, we are speaking
to their body to begin the healing process and return to normal;
this is where we use (quote) the Word. The Bible is full of verses
that we can use. Memorize at least four or five.

We **speak** words of authority. We **command** others to obey.

Command or Speak – There is a big difference.

Joshua spoke to the sun and it stood still. The Lord told Moses
to speak to the rock and it would give forth water but instead he
struck the rock (natural authority instead of spiritual).

Jesus gave to His Disciples – Authority. This is a God given
right because of our citizenship in the Kingdom of God. In the
natural or physical, authority alone is great as long as we meet
people who will comply or obey that authority; that do not
question our authority. However, there are situations where it is
only when we exercise power, that others will comply.

A uniform and badge of a police officer represent his
authority; but the gun represents his power. However, some will
surrender to his power only when his gun is drawn.

All believers have authority (see level of Authority above).
Not all believers, however, have the power to command. To be

able to command means you have the ability to back up what you speak. It means you either have the power yourself or you have right to use the power of others.

We are merely human beings therefore; we have no power of our own except our physical strength. Since ministry is spiritual, our power must be spiritual. The only power that is available to us is the power of the Holy Spirit.

When Jesus was addressing demons, evil spirits or unclean spirits He sometimes spoke and at other times, He commanded. The weaker demons responded to His authority and stronger spirits responded to His command. Stronger spirits do not obey unless they feel threatened by a worst situation than they are already in.

Even with Jesus, His power came from the Holy Spirit.

Some Scripture to memorize:

- *Therefore submit to God. Resist the devil and he will flee from you. James 4:7*

- *Be sober, be vigilant; because your adversary the devil walks about like a roaring lion, seeking whom he may devour. Resist him, steadfast in the faith, knowing that the same sufferings are experienced by your brotherhood in the world. 1 Peter 5:8-9*

- *He has delivered us from the power of darkness and conveyed us into the kingdom of the Son of His love, Col 1:13-14*

- *Having disarmed principalities and powers, He made a public spectacle of them, triumphing over them in it. Col 2:15*

- *"Be angry, and do not sin": do not let the sun go down on your wrath, nor give place to the devil. Eph 4:26-28*

- *For though we walk in the flesh, we do not war according to the flesh. For the weapons of our warfare are not carnal but mighty in God for pulling down strongholds, casting down arguments and every high thing that exalts itself against the knowledge of God, bringing every thought into captivity to the obedience of Christ, 2 Cor 10:3-6*

- *How God anointed Jesus of Nazareth with the Holy Spirit and with power, who went about doing good and healing all who were oppressed by the devil, for God was with Him. Acts 10:38-39*

- *Put on the whole armor of God, that you may be able to stand against the wiles of the devil. For we do not wrestle against flesh and blood, but against principalities, against powers, against the rulers of the darkness of this age, against spiritual hosts of wickedness in the heavenly places. Eph 6:11-12*

- *And they overcame him by the blood of the Lamb and by the word of their testimony, and they did not love their lives to the death. Rev 12:11-12*

"BE FILLED WITH THE HOLY SPIRIT"

Why was it so imperative that they wait for this Promise?

Was it imperative that they wait? Jesus thought so. Listen to what He said in various translations of Acts 1:4

- *And being assembled together with them, **He commanded** them not to depart from Jerusalem, but to wait for the Promise of the Father, NKJV*

- *And, being assembled together with them, **commanded them** that they should not depart from Jerusalem, but wait for the promise of the Father, KJV*

- *On one occasion, while he was eating with them, **he gave them this command:** "Do not leave Jerusalem, but wait for the gift my Father promised, NIV*

- *And while staying with them **he charged them** not to depart from Jerusalem, but to wait for the promise of the Father, RSV*

- *being assembled with [them], **commanded them** not to depart from Jerusalem, but to await the promise of the Father, Darby*

We have to understand why it was so important to God that these disciples receive the fulfillment of the Father's Promise. Although Jesus had triumphed over the Devil and destroyed his works, it is only as the Church fully develops its relationship with

Him (bearing His image) and then using His authority and power that they will be able to do the things that please the Father and extend His Kingdom to the whole Earth.

John tells us that when they believed in Jesus as the Son of God, the Father gave them power to become the Children of God. However, God was not satisfied that they remain children. Just as Jesus grew in wisdom and in stature with God and man, so must they. The Father had a Grand Plan for them that was beyond their wildest imagination. His Grand Plan was for them was to mature into a son, like unto Jesus the first born that they might rule and reign with Him.

In order for Jesus to accomplish his mission, He emptied himself of the power that He had as God's Word in Heaven, took on the form of a man, and became a servant. As a man, He was now limited to the constraints of time, space and human ability. He was subject to his parents, His teachers, His elders, the culture, and the authorities. When Jesus was growing up, He was no different from any of the other kids on the block except for one thing; He had the abiding presence of the Holy Spirit with him. While on Earth, Jesus always enjoyed His relationship with God because His heart was righteous and there was no sin found within Him. The Holy Spirit was with him from the beginning of his life.

However, when it became time for Jesus to start his earthly ministry, He knew that it was not by power, not by might but by the Holy Spirit. He sought out John the Baptist who had been told, *'Upon whom you see the Spirit descending, and remaining on Him, this is He who baptizes with the Holy Spirit.' And I have seen and testified that this is the Son of God."* Jesus learned obedience from suffering (dying to self) just as you and I must. Self must die and give way to obedience to the Father and like Jesus, be able to say, "Not my will but yours be done".

Therefore, Jesus, who had been given the responsibility to reclaim the Father's Kingdom and redeem humanity from the wrath of God; waited until the time was set for Him to receive power from on high that He might go forth and proclaim that the Kingdom had come. We can only imagine the joy and excitement that must have been in Jesus' heart when the Holy Spirit descended and came upon Him. He had been looking upon humanity with all their hurts, pains and sorrows. Now He was able to do something about it. Acts 2; 33

Luke tells us that, Jesus, having been led into the wilderness by the Holy Spirit, was tempted for forty days and upon returning victorious (having not sinned), He went to the synagogue. All eyes were fixed upon him as He opened the book and found the place where it was written, *"The Spirit of the Lord is upon me, because he has anointed me to preach the good news to the poor. He has sent me to proclaim release to the captives and recovering of sight to the blind, to set at liberty those who are oppressed."* He then sat down and told them, *"This saying is NOW fulfilled"*.

Without this power, that was wrapped up in the Promise of the father, all His words would be only a man's word and of no avail, no benefit. God said this about His Word in Isa 55:11, *"So shall My word be that goes forth from My mouth; It shall not return to Me void, But it shall accomplish what I please, And it shall prosper in the thing for which I sent it."* Jesus is the word sent from God. Without the power of the Holy Spirit, however, it would have been the same for Him just as it was for Moses when he first tried to redeem his people in Egypt; failure.

We have been given a mission, and to perform our task we must have power. Since it does not reside within us as human beings, we must ask for it. Power resides in the Being of the Holy Spirit, therefore, we need the Baptism in the Holy Spirit and we must wait upon the Lord, as He is the giver. Waiting is not meant for us to wait for a specific time; waiting is for us to allow God to create a hunger, desire, and brokenness within us before we receive such an awesome gift. The word "wait" is synonymous with "hope".

What did Jesus see, even before He started His ministry? What is it that we must see as well if we are to be effective in our ministry? *"And He said to them, "I saw Satan fall like lightning from heaven. Behold, I give you the authority to trample on serpents and scorpions, and over all the power of the enemy, and nothing shall by any means hurt you."* Luke 10:17-20

121

Chapter 7
Who can be Healed?

GOD WANTS TO HEAL YOU!

The heart of compassion that we display toward others comes from our Father. It is part of His nature and as His children; it is a part of our new nature. This compassion is even affecting the ungodly without their knowing it. Our Creator has even put within the conscience of the ungodly to help the helpless. They think that it is just part of being human to care for the weak, when, in reality; their Creator is their motivator.

Central and at the very heart of the matter of healing, is this question: Do you believe that God wants to heal YOU? Can you see the Love that in is His heart for you? Do you have a relationship close enough that you can say that you trust Him?

Can you believe that God wants to heal you? How do you handle headaches, backaches, rashes, pains, flu, Cancer, diabetes, high blood pressure, arthritis, kidney infection, or stroke? Is it your first thought to run to the drug store, medicine cabinet, or the doctor? On the other hand, have you come to the point were you believe there is no cure for you?

Can you accept into your spirit the following statement? If you do not have faith that you can receive healing in your body then you cannot receive healing. The same can be said for the healing of others for whom you pray. You must settle this first in your own spirit, heart and mind.

A KINGDOM WHICH CANNOT BE SHAKEN

Before you can trust anyone, even God, you must answer three questions: (1) does the person making the promise have the ability to do what they say, (2) do they have the desire to do as they say, and (3) if the above two are yes, then will they carry out what they say; are they faithful to their word?

Do you have doubts? Doubt is the killer of faith. If you have any doubts whether or not God wants to heal you, perfect faith cannot exist and until you apply faith, you will not be healed.

Here are three scriptures that tell us so:

- *But without faith it is impossible to please Him, for he who comes to God must believe that He is, and that He is a rewarder of those who diligently seek Him. Heb 11:6*

- *But let him ask in faith, with no doubting, for he who doubts is like a wave of the sea driven and tossed by the wind. For let not that man suppose that he will receive anything from the Lord; he is a double-minded man, unstable in all his ways. James 1:6-8*

- *But he who doubts is condemned if he eats, because he does not eat from faith; for whatever is not from faith is sin. Rom 14:23*

If we believe that God keeps His Word in other aspects of our life, why can we not believe that God will keep His Word regarding healing? We must know that God does keep his Word whether the promise is for salvation, protection, provision, or healing. He is faithful to his Word. God does not lie. The god of this world is the liar and is the father of lies.

Under the old covenant, God's people were healed when they believed what God said, and then acted on it. Under the new covenant, based on the life, death and resurrection of Jesus, we have even better promises. Jesus fulfilled God's Word in the Old Testament and the New Testament.

Before we go further, let us ask ourselves a few questions and apply them to healing!

- Is there anything in my shoebox? Introduction

- How tightly packed are the jellybeans in my jar? Chapter 1, BORN TO RULE

124

- Have I accepted a Kingdom Worldview? Chapter 2, BORN TO RULE

- Am I walking down the Narrow Way, the Way of the Internal Cross? Chapter 5, BORN TO RULE

- Has my faith expanded beyond Predeterminism?

- Am I relying on the Holy Spirit to reveal to me the truth regarding healing?

We must approach our explanation of Scripture with the reliance upon the Holy Spirit. We must approach Scripture not purely from an intellectual standpoint, but from our Father's point of view. If we look to the Holy Spirit to reveal only the meaning of words, it would be like looking at a painting and trying to know what was in the artist heart by the color of the paint and the type of strokes he is using. We must get the meaning from the artist himself if we are to know the true meaning. The Holy Spirit is the one that reveals the Father's heart for He has been with the Father from the beginning.

We need to look at sickness and disease the same way the Father looks at it: how it affects His children for whom his son died. Since all truth is parallel, how do you view sickness that attacks and destroys your children or your loved ones? Do we not spend Billions of dollars every year to alleviate the pain and the trauma of sickness? Would we not take the pain ourselves for our small children, our babies if we could? Could our heavenly Father look at sickness, disease and pain in any other way different from us?

We have also fervently emphasized the need to study, meditate on, and to live the Word of God. Our study must include the whole counsel of God. We must stand back and get a proper perspective by starting at the proper starting point, the Father's heart.

GOD'S WORD -THE BASIS OF YOUR FAITH

The seed, planted by the farmer, is like God's Word. The farmer plants a seed, in faith, that he will in due time reap a harvest. The soil, the amount of water, the amount of sun, and the quality of this seed itself, all play a role in the lack or the plenty of the harvest. Still the farmer plants the seed. He trusts God for the harvest.

Rom 1:16 says, *"The Word of God is powerful unto salvation"*. The Bible says that, *"God sent his word to heal them."* Psalms 107: 19, 20

Our basis for faith for our healing is God's Word. The Bible tells us that Jesus came to do the will of the Father. He healed all that came to him believing. If Jesus did the will of the Father then, why is it so hard for us to believe that we can receive healing now, *"Jesus is the same yesterday, today, and forever."* Heb 13:8

If we believe that salvation, healing, and deliverance, is for all, then we can pray the prayer of faith. "Whosoever", "as many will" means, that the invitation to come into the kingdom to be saved and healed is for everyone. We are finding out, however, that this invitation must be sounded in the Church as well as out in the highways and byways.

A Word Study

In the Greek, the word "saved" is sozo (sode'-zo); from a primary "sos" (contraction for obsolete "saoz", "safe"); to save, i.e. deliver or protect (literally or figuratively):

Our Bibles render this word - heal, preserve, save (self), do well, be (make) whole. The highly respected Vines Expository Dictionary of New Testament Words says these words are used in a variety of ways: Of material and temporal deliverance from danger, suffering, etc.; from sickness; of the spiritual and eternal salvation granted

126

"and begged Him earnestly, saying, "My little daughter lies at the point of death. Come and lay Your hands on her, that she may be (sozo) **healed,** *and she will live." Mark 5:23*

"praising God and having favor with all the people. And the Lord added to the church daily those who were being (sozo) **saved".** *Acts 2:47*

Jesus came to redeem the whole person, not just the soul. The whole person includes both the spiritual and the physical. If we separate the two, we do not have a whole human being. 1 Peter 2:24 says, *" who Himself bore our sins in His own body on the tree, that we, having died to sins, might live for righteousness — by whose stripes you were healed."* Here the word (iaomai) *"healed" comes from the Greek - to cure, to heal, to be made whole.* Also in Acts 10:38 the Greek word (iaomai) is translated "healed" and generally refers to physical healing.

1 John 2:18 tells us that, *"Jesus came to destroy the works of the devil".* Luke 4:18 says He came to set the captives free, to save the loss and He came to make known the mercy, grace, love, and the power of God. He saves, heals and delivers all that come to Him in faith. "As many", "whosoever", "all", are welcome to receive.

Are you a believer? Can you help others to believe? Jesus said, *"according to your faith, be it unto you".* What would you receive, "according to your faith", anything? Do you have great faith when dealing with healing or is there little or maybe no faith?

Faith comes by HEARING the Word of God. It does not come from someone else or from some other book. Faith, to receive healing, will come when we know what the Word of God says on the subject and allow it to transform our spirit.

Matthew 9:35

Jesus went through all the towns and villages, teaching in their synagogues, preaching the good news of the kingdom and **healing every disease and sickness.** *NIV*

Matthew 12:15

Aware of this, Jesus withdrew from that place. Many followed him, and **he healed all their sick,** *NIV*

127

THE CROSS AND HEALING?

If we are to have Faith for healing, we must answer these six questions: 1. Does Jesus dispense healing the same as a Doctor dispenses medicine or a surgeon performs an operation? NO. Is he selective with whom he heals? NO. Is there something else that reduces healing down to a common denominator? NO. Is there a one-time act of God that allows people, regardless of their culture, sex, intelligence, or age to receive healing? YES. Is there something that God did that allows us to receive healing, the same way we received salvation-through faith? YES. Is there healing in the atonement? YES.

When we speak of the Atonement, we mean, "to give or do that whereby alienation ceases and reconciliation ensues" (Fausset's Bible Dictionary, Copyright (c) 1998, 2003 by Biblesoft). In other words, the settlement of the hostility between you and God has been finalized.

In the Atonement, reconciliation inserts itself between the Believer and the wrath of God. In the Old Testament, the sacrifice of animals atoned for the offender's sin and turned aside God's wrath.

The Book of Isaiah plays an important role in the prediction of the life and ministry of the Promised Messiah; therefore let us examine it a little more closely. We must note that the Prophet Isaiah was looking several hundred years into the future.

Isaiah 53 says:

He has no form or Comeliness; and when we see Him,
There is no beauty that we should desire Him. He is despised and rejected by men,
A Man of sorrows and acquainted with grief. In addition, we hid, as it were, our faces from Him;
He was despised, and we did not esteem Him.
Surely, He has borne our griefs and carried our sorrows; yet we esteemed Him stricken, Smitten by God, and afflicted.
But He was wounded for our transgressions,
He was bruised for our iniquities; The chastisement for our peace was upon Him, And by His stripes we are healed.

As Isaiah looks in on this scene, the Holy Spirit reveals that the Messiah fulfills the Atonement as typified by the sacrificing of the one goat for the sin offering and the other goat as the scapegoat. Isaiah also includes; the Messiah has also borne our griefs (sickness) and carried our sorrows (pains).

From Leviticus 16:20-22, we can consider the ceremonial offering of the two goats as the make up of one typical sin offering, which is exhibited in two significant points of view. The transfer of the sins of the people to the sacrificial goat was symbolized by the laying on of hands of the Jewish high priest. After the slaughter of the goat, the blood was taken into the inner sanctuary to be sprinkled before the Lord, therefore foreshadowing the sacrifice of the Messiah who would take away the sin of the world.

Since the people could not witness the acts of the high priest in the Most Holy Place, the scapegoat was ordered that the removal of their sins might be made visible as it were to their bodily eyes, and they might be convinced that when God forgives, He also forgets. Like the goat that was sacrificed, their sins were collectively transferred to the head of the scapegoat, which was never more to be seen having been led into the wilderness before them all.

Isaiah makes it clear who the Messiah is dying for and why, by saying, "But he was wounded for **our** transgressions, He was bruised for **our** iniquities and the chastisement for **our** peace was upon Him". He did not die for His sin (he had no sin); He was dying for our sin. He is taking upon himself our sin and receiving our due punishment, that we might receive PEACE and be forgiven. Isaiah points out to us that as part of this atonement, we are healed.

To make sense of the above we need to look at four Hebrew words. In the KJV the Hebrew word (choli) is translated as *griefs*, yet in the majority of uses in the OT it is translated *disease*. Similarly, the Hebrew word (makob) is translated *sorrows*, yet in the majority of uses in the OT, it is translated *pain*.

129

Isaiah 53:4 could read, "Surely he has borne our sicknesses and carried our pains". Even Matthew clarifies this when he says in Matt 8:16-18.

When evening had come, they brought to Him many who were demon-possessed. And He cast out the spirits with a word, and healed all who were sick, that it might be fulfilled which was spoken by Isaiah the prophet, saying: "He Himself took our infirmities and bore our sicknesses."

The two additional verbs are found in Isaiah 53:7 where we see the Hebrew words, borne (*nasa*) and carried (*cabal*). *Nasa* means to bear in the sense of suffering punishment for something as seen in Lev 5:1, "*If a person sins...he bears guilt*". Here the emphasis is on the bearing of it away. The Hebrew word *Cabal* also means to bear the punishment but the emphasis is on the weight of the load.

The thought here is the Messiah would bear the full weight of the sin of the world and would carry them away never to be dealt with again. In order words, there would never need to be another sacrifice for sin.

In Hebrew thought, there is no sharp distinction between diseases of the body and those of the soul. All sickness was taken to be the consequence of sin.

This passage in Isaiah 53 is universally recognized as pertaining to Calvary and is a picture of Jesus as He endured the cross in order to reconcile us to the Father. Isaiah reveals that not only was Jesus the Lamb that was slain in order for us to receive Forgiveness and find peace in our soul, but that also we might be healed in our body. 2 Cor. 5:21 tells us that Jesus "*was made sin who knew no sin to be sin for us, that we might become the righteousness of God in Him*".

We have already looked at the Greek word (*sozo*). We stated that it is sometimes translated *healed* and sometimes *saved*. The whole person is saved through the atoning act of Jesus. We have been redeemed from the penalty of sin and we have been redeemed from the curse of sickness and disease.

Hundreds of years earlier, King David prophesizes regarding the benefits to follow the death and resurrection of Jesus. Psalms 103:1-5 tell of the benefits that belong to those that are part of the family of the God.

However, it is verse 3 that puts forgiveness and healing together; *"Who forgives all your iniquities, Who heals all your disease".*

1 Peter 2:23-24 also brings them together when he says, *"For to this you were called, because Christ also suffered for us, leaving us an example, that you should follow His steps: "Who committed no sin, Nor was deceit found in His mouth"; who, when He was reviled, did not revile in return; when He suffered, He did not threaten, but committed Himself to Him who judges righteously; who Himself bore our sins in His own body on the tree, that we, having died to sins, might live for righteousness — by whose stripes you were healed.*

Even Paul writes and tells us that Jesus took the curse of our sin upon Himself. *Christ has redeemed us from the curse of the law, having become a curse for us (for it is written, "Cursed is everyone who hangs on a tree"), that the blessing of Abraham might come upon the Gentiles in Christ Jesus, that we might receive the promise of the Spirit through faith Gal 3: 13.* Sickness and disease are a part of the curse.

The Bible says; if we are sons, then we are heirs of God, through Jesus Christ. We are heirs of all the promises of God. Jesus paid the penalty for our sin, and once the penalty was paid, there remained no more accusations and no more effects of the curse. Once a convicted thief, murder, or whatever has paid his price to society for his crime, he is set free from its curse.

THIS IS THE FACT: **we are freed from the curse.**

The work of the cross is a finished work. We do not (even dare not) ask Jesus to do another thing. Jesus said on the Cross: "IT IS FINISHED". Because of this, Faith looks back to an accomplished work and Hope looks forward to the possibility or the fulfillment of the promise.

We cannot have blind faith. There must be a basis for faith. This basis for our faith is; the finished work of Jesus on the Cross.

There is certainty in faith; there is confidence, assurance, trust. Therefore, when faith is there, there is also peace. This peace is given and we know, that we know, that we know that we have the things that we have asked for. See 1 John 5:15, 16

Faith does not need encouragement from the five senses. Faith is not swayed by what the eyes see, or the ears hear or the pain felt or not felt. It is settled upon the word of God. Faith draws its strengths from the Word of God and faith gives honor to the Word of God. Jesus is the Word and the Word became flesh. God sent his Word and he healed them.

Other Considerations

The medical profession has long known the fact that roughly 75% of all illnesses are psychosomatic. Proverbs gives us insight into this by saying that, *"A merry heart does good, like medicine, but a broken spirit dries the bones".* Proverbs 17:22   Other Scriptures that inform us:

* *Anxiety in the heart of man causes depression, but a good word makes it glad.*

* *A merry heart makes a cheerful countenance, but by sorrow of the heart the spirit is broken.*

* *The spirit of a man will sustain him in sickness, but who can bear a broken spirit?*

* *A sound heart is life to the body, but envy is rottenness to the bones. All the days of the afflicted are evil,   but he who is of a merry heart has a continual feast.*

* *The light of the eyes rejoices the heart, And a good report makes the bones healthy.*

* *When you see this, your heart shall rejoice, and your bones shall flourish like grass; the hand of the Lord shall be known to His servants, and His indignation to His enemies. Isa 66:14*

We might ask about those that have the Gift of Healing. Why don't they just go into the hospitals and heal all those that are sick? Why is it that not all are healed? Answer - Neither salvation nor healing can be prayed down from heaven, nor can we persuade God to do anything. He has already done what needs to be done. It is finished. We are healed by grace through faith.

You are not healed because you feel healed or the pain has subsided. You are healed because of the finished work of the Cross. It is finished. By his stripes, you are healed. A person whose is sick must have the faith that; IT IS FINISHED. If not, they cannot be healed. This is why someone with the Gift of healing cannot go into a hospital and just begin praying for the sick that they might all be healed. The recipient must have a measure of faith.

HEALING SCRIPTURES

God's Intentional Will Is Health

*My son, pay attention to what I say; listen closely to my words. Do not let them out of your sight, keep them within your heart; for they are life to those who find them and **health to a man's whole body**.* NIV Proverbs 4:20-22

*Dear friend, I pray that you may **enjoy good health** and that all may go well with you, even as your soul is getting along well.* NIV 3 John 2

*But I **will restore you to health** and heal your wounds, declares the LORD, 'because you are called an outcast, Zion for whom no one cares.'* NIV Jeremiah 30:17

*"'Nevertheless, I **will bring health and healing** to it; I will heal my people and will let them enjoy abundant peace and security.* NIV Jeremiah 33:6

*Then your light will break forth like the dawn, and **your healing will quickly appear**; then your righteousness will go before you, and the glory of the LORD will be your rear guard.* NIV Isaiah 58:8

*May God himself, the God of peace, sanctify you through and through. May your whole spirit, soul and body **be kept blameless** at the coming of our Lord Jesus Christ.* NIV 1 Thessalonians 5:23

The Word Brings Health

*When evening came, many who were demon-possessed were brought to him, and he **drove out the spirits with a word** and healed all the sick.* NIV Matthew 8:16

In the beginning was the Word, and the Word was with God, and the Word was God. The Word became flesh and made his dwelling among us. We have seen his glory, the glory of the One and Only, who came from the Father, full of grace and truth. NIV John 1:1

*He **sent forth his word and healed them**; he rescued them from the grave.* NIV Psalms 107:20

*so **is my word that goes out from my mouth**: It will not return to me empty, but will accomplish what I desire and achieve the purpose for which I sent it.* NIV Isaiah 55:11

Prayer Brings Healing

*This is the confidence we have in approaching God: that **if we ask anything according to his will**, he hears us. And if we know that he hears us-whatever we ask-we know that we have what we asked of him.* NIV   1 John 5:14-15

*And I will do **whatever you ask in my name**, so that the Son may bring glory to the Father. 14 **You may ask me for anything in my name, and I will do it**.* NIV John 14:13-14

*In that day you will no longer ask me anything. I tell you the truth, **my Father will give you whatever you ask in my name.** Until now you have not asked for anything in my name. Ask and you will receive, and your joy will be complete.* NIV John 16:23-24

Chaper 8
Spiritual Warfare

Our heavenly Father's intention was and is still today, to extend His kingdom (Domain) from the invisible to the visible – from the Spiritual realm to the Physical realm. His original plan was and still is to have man be his agent on earth and let him have dominion over all He created.

However, because man rebelled against God's rule, he thereby relinquished his place of authority. He left his place of safety under the rule of God and by his own violation, placed himself under the rule of Satan. Because man lost dominion over His kingdom, God put into motion a plan (formed before the foundation the earth) that would enable Himself to re-claim His kingdom and restore Man to his first position of having dominion over the earth. It was given to Man the responsibility, however, to extend the kingdom or repopulate the earth with heavenly citizens.

Jesus was passionate about reclaiming His Father's Kingdom and destroying the works of His enemy. If we are not just as passionate in our fight we will consider Satan and his demons, not as enemies, but only as opponents. When this happens we will not be victorious.

SPIRIT WARFARE IS NOT AN OPTION

God's plan included the removal of Satan as, "god of this world" and "prince of the air". God removed Satan from his position of stolen authority; reclaimed His Kingdom and restored man to his former position of authority. This authority is not original to man's nature but comes only as man maintains his relationship with God through His Son, Christ Jesus. God's re-establishment of His kingdom is tied therefore, to Man's reconciliation unto Himself. This fact of God's love should overwhelm the heart of every believer and follower of Christ.

Before man is restored to a place of dominion, he must first be reconciled to the Father. It was for this cause that Jesus bore the sins of all and endured the shame of the cross. Jesus' motivation for coming to earth was not just to "save us" from sin (that is the goal of religion), but to bring "heaven's rule to man". What is known as the Lord's Prayer includes this phrase, "Thy kingdom come thy will be done on earth as it is in heaven". This one sentence announces God's promise and His intent to wage warfare against Satan to reclaim and restore His Kingdom, as well as proclaim the resultant victory.

When we go out to give our "witness" to those that do not know God the Father, it is to bring them into the kingdom while they are living, NOT to get them into heaven when they die. To do this we must enter into Spiritual Warfare.

Biblical description of Our Warfare

The Bible mentions the Promise Land and Heaven. It is important for us to understand that they are not the same place. The Promise land is the Promise Land and Heaven is Heaven. Heaven is a spiritual place, an invisible place. For the Jews, the Promise Land was the land now known as Israel. For us here in America it might be the land of the United States. This is our promise land and we are to go forth and conquer (take it away from the enemy) and rule over it as God intended, in peace and

136

righteousness. However, for Christian's in general, the Promise Land is the whole Earth.

When Israel went into their Promised Land, they faced seven nations greater and mightier than themselves, but they were not to be afraid. Deut 7:1-5 reveals God's foreknowledge regarding their enemies and the instructions that they must follow in order that they may continue in their relationship and be blessed.

*"When the Lord your God brings you into the land which you go to possess, and has cast out many nations before you, the Hittites and the Girgashites and the Amorites and the Canaanites and the Perizzites and the Hivites and the Jebusites, **seven nations greater and mightier than you**, and when the Lord your God delivers them over to you, you shall conquer them and utterly destroy them. You shall make no covenant with them nor show mercy to them.*

Nor shall you make marriages with them. You shall not give your daughter to their son, nor take their daughter for your son. For they will turn your sons away from following Me, to serve other gods; so the anger of the Lord will be aroused against you and destroy you suddenly. But thus you shall deal with them: you shall destroy their altars, and break down their sacred pillars, and cut down their wooden images, and burn their carved images with fire". KJV Emphasis mine

FROM DISCIPLE TO WARRIOR

Jesus said He is the door or the gate into the kingdom. Because of our Faith in the Work of the Cross, we enter in and once we are in the Kingdom, the Holy Spirit begins His transformation process and forms Christ in us. From here, as we mature, we go on to become an Overcomer, ministering to those in need, inside and outside of the Kingdom; bringing the love and power of our King to them; healing the sick, casting out demons and mending their broken hearts; extending the God's Kingdom.

As an Overcomer, we begin taking back what - the Devil has stolen; taking back our society: our local government, media, arts (including entertainment and sports), books, families, education, commerce, science and technology, and our peace. It is time to be a Warrior for Christ.

The Promised Land is not in the "Here After"; it is here, right here – the entire earth. We are to go forth and conquer it, have dominion over it, rule it. There are giants in the land. There are principalities, powers, rulers of darkness in the land. However, praise God, Jesus is the King and has all authority over heaven and earth and He says to us, GO FORTH AND OVERCOME.

We are however, a much divided people, in and outside the Church. Our Worldviews separate us until schisms break forth and we stand on two sides of a great divide. We have visions for our "Promised Land" that others in our culture do not share. There is a constant collision of mindsets - (road maps for attitudes and behavior), of value systems, and visions for the future.

The Apostle Paul was exposed to different cultures in his missionary journeys so he was uniquely qualified to express the battleground. He wrote in II Corinthians 10:4-5, *"For the weapons of our warfare are not carnal but mighty in God for pulling down strongholds, casting down arguments and every high thing that exalts itself against the knowledge of God, bringing every thought into captivity to the obedience of Christ..."*

It is a spiritual battle in the mind. Even the Bible tells us, "for who can know the thoughts of a man except God and the man himself" So it is, WE who know God and the power of His resurrection, that are called upon to do battle against the enemies of God. If we sit idly by and are passive in our actions, it will be as horrified spectators watching our "Promised Land" slide deeper and deeper into darkness. At the end, if we do not act, we will have to give an account for our lack of action when the King of Kings has given us power over our enemies and the authority to command even principalities, powers and rulers of darkness to flee in the name of Jesus.

We see it so clearly when we think of a father and his son or daughter who is being assailed by an evil person. The LOVE of the father cause righteous indignation to rise up and then his POWER is released to overcome the oppressor. This LOVE and POWER go together to win the battle.

When Israel was brought out of Egypt, God's LOVE for His people caused His POWER to be revealed against Israel's enemies that they might win the battle and obtain the prize, the Promised Land. God's Power was released by Faith then and it is still that way today.

BATTLEFRONTS

There are three (3) battlefronts we must acknowledged if we are going to win the victory over Satan. The first battlefront is for the affections of a man's heart and the second is for the blessings that God has promised to him. The third is related to the other two – we are to make God's name known throughout the whole Earth.

Regarding the **FIRST**, man's affection: God said that man is to LOVE God and worship only Him. Jesus addresses this when speaking to the woman at the well. He said, *"Woman, believe Me, the hour is coming when you will neither on this mountain, nor in Jerusalem, worship the Father. You worship what you do not know; we know what we worship, for salvation is of the Jews. But the hour is coming, and now is, when the true worshipers will worship the Father in spirit and truth; for the Father is seeking such to worship Him. God is Spirit, and those who worship Him must worship in spirit and truth."* "John 4:21-24

Adam Clark, in his commentary on John 4:24 said this; "As all creatures were made by him, so all owe him obedience and reverence. Nevertheless, to be acceptable to this infinite Spirit, the worship must be of a spiritual nature-must spring from the heart, through the influence of the Holy Spirit: and it must be in TRUTH, not only in sincerity, but performed according to that divine revelation which he has given men of himself.

A man worships God in spirit, when, under the influence of the Holy Spirit, he brings all his affections, appetites, and desires to the throne of God; and he worships him in truth, when every purpose and passion of his heart, and when every act of his religious worship, is guided and regulated by the word of God."

We must win the hearts of men (not convince them that they are a sinner) by exhibiting the presence of the Spirit. His love must flow through us, not just in doing good and showing kindness but also in POWER. We must believe that the power of the Holy Spirit will be there to convict of Sin, Righteousness, and Judgment. We must believe that the Presence of God also means, the Power of God.

People love the flesh, love self, the seen rather than the unseen, therefore, as we go out to preach the gospel to the Gospel of the Kingdom, we must go with the anointing just as Jesus went with the anointing. We must have the Word of God ready to speak for it is the Word that is anointed.

Regarding the **SECOND,** Jesus said, *"Do not fear, little flock, for it is your Father's good pleasure to give you the kingdom".* This is the Father's desire for His children; give them the Kingdom. Satan does not want you or me to know this and will use deception and lies to keep us in ignorance.

This Battlefront is tied with the first because it affects those that have entered into the Kingdom. Those that have entered the Kingdom come with their sicknesses, oppressions, their hurts and pains and their strongholds that cause them to have Worldviews that are self-centered. If they are to grow in their faith and mature in their walk with the Lord of lords and the King of kings, they must be healed, delivered and set free from those things that so easily beset them (Heb 12:1).

The battle starts in our own life. If we are to proclaim the glory of the Lord, we must first experience it. If we are to proclaim that with God nothing is impossible; if we are to proclaim that He can set the captive free, we must experience that freedom ourselves and have witnessed the miracles ourselves. If we say that Jesus is the great physician, we must have experienced His healing touch ourselves. **We are to be witnesses, not tellers of truths that come to us secondhand.** See Acts 1:8

Now to the **THIRD** – making God's Name known: *"And what one nation in the earth is like thy people, even like Israel, whom God went to redeem for a people to himself, and to make a name, and to do for you great things and terrible, for thy land..." 2 Sam 7:23.*

106 times throughout the Bible, God says, "shall know". He wanted the people of Israel "to know". He wanted the Egyptians "to know". He wanted all the nations of the earth "to know". He wanted all "to know" that He is God alone and that He is the God of His "People".

God was going to be known for his "mighty acts". It was the responsibility of the Nation of Israel to proclaim His mighty acts among the nations. It was their responsibility to make His Name known to all the peoples of the Earth. It was their responsibility to be a blessing to all God's creation by living in His Presence and in His Power.

Listen to what David proclaims in Ps 145:1-13

"I will extol You, my God, O King; and I will bless Your name forever and ever. Every day I will bless You, and I will praise Your name forever and ever. Great is the Lord, and greatly to be praised; and His greatness is unsearchable.

ONE GENERATION SHALL PRAISE YOUR WORKS TO ANOTHER, AND SHALL DECLARE YOUR MIGHTY ACTS. I will meditate on the glorious splendor of Your majesty, and on Your wondrous works. MEN SHALL SPEAK OF THE MIGHT OF YOUR AWESOME ACTS AND I WILL DECLARE YOUR GREATNESS. They shall utter the memory of Your great goodness, and shall sing of Your righteousness.

The Lord is gracious and full of compassion, Slow to anger and great in mercy. The Lord is good to all, and His tender mercies are over all His works. All Your works shall praise You, O Lord, and Your saints shall bless You. THEY SHALL SPEAK OF THE GLORY OF YOUR KINGDOM, AND TALK OF YOUR POWER, To make known to the sons of men His mighty acts, and the glorious majesty of His kingdom. Your kingdom is an everlasting kingdom, and Your dominion endures throughout all generations". Emphasis author's

SPIRIT BAPTISM

The Baptism in the Holy Spirit has been an area of contention for the last 100 years. I believe the reason is that there has been a concentration on the "experience", rather then on the true purpose. Pentecostal and Charismatic churches have focused on the "experience" and have left the Saint feeling, "Wow, I got it" but then they know nothing of doing anything with this power. They have not used this power to proclaim the Gospel of the Kingdom of God and extend the Kingdom, as it should have done.

WHAT THE PRESENT DAY CHURCH HAS FORGOTTEN IS; IT IS NOT ABOUT THE EXPERIENCE, IT HAS ALWAYS BEEN ABOUT THE POWER TO COMPLETE THE "TASK AT HAND".

When we look at the hall of fame of God's leaders, we see people like Moses, Sampson, Othniel, Jephthah, Gideon, King David, and the prophets Elijah and, Elisha. We see men, having an experience with "power", but that was NOT their objective. Their objective was – to get the job done that God had given them to do.

The early Disciples knew this; the question is, do we? Listen to what the Bible says when Peter and John came out from prison for speaking in the Name of Jesus, *"And being let go, they went to their own companions and reported all that the chief priests and elders had said to them. So when they heard that, they raised their voice to God with one accord and said: "Lord, You are God, who made heaven and earth and the sea, and all that is in them, who by the mouth of Your servant David have said:*

'Why did the nations rage, And the people plot vain things? The kings of the earth took their stand, And the rulers were gathered together against the Lord and against His Christ.'

"For truly against Your holy Servant Jesus, whom You anointed, both Herod and Pontius Pilate, with the Gentiles and the people of Israel, were gathered together to do whatever Your hand and Your purpose determined before to be done.

Now, Lord, look on their threats, and grant to Your servants that with all boldness they may speak Your word, by stretching out Your hand to heal, and that signs and wonders may be done through the name of Your holy Servant Jesus."

And when they had prayed, the place where they were assembled together was shaken; and they were all filled with the Holy Spirit, and they spoke the word of God with boldness. Acts 4:23-31

We can ask the same question today as did Peter, "Why did the nations rage, and the people plot ineffective, worthless things? Even today, nations are plotting against the Church of the Lord Jesus Christ. However, they do not realize that it is a losing battle.

Nevertheless, just because we know who wins does not mean that we can sit back and not be involved. It is because of our involvement that we do win. As people of the light, we do not seek to escape but to run to the battle.

It is because of our involvement in the battle that we ask for the Baptism in the Holy Spirit. Luke writes of this wonderful promise given by Jesus, when He says, *"If a son asks for bread from any father among you, will he give him a stone? Or if he asks for a fish, will he give him a serpent instead of a fish? Or if he asks for an egg, will he offer him a scorpion? If you then, being evil, know how to give good gifts to your children, how much more will your heavenly Father give the Holy Spirit to those who ask Him."* Luke 11:11-13

It was always about the task given. It was the completion of the task, which gave sense to the words spoken by Jesus regarding the parable of the Talents, "Well done good and faithful servant".

It was never about an "experience" of being Baptized in the Holy Spirit. It was about, "What do I need in order to get the job done?" Jesus was baptized in the Holy Spirit because He was fully man and without the Power of the Holy Spirit, He could not fulfill His task. He needed POWER. The early Disciples had a job to do; they needed to be Baptized in the Holy Spirit to receive power. We have a job to do, the same job as the early Disciples. Do we think we can do it without the POWER?

In the first book we said, "Glory is given only when the person or thing does what it was created to do. The sun and the moon have their own unique glory. If the sun stopped shining or the moon stopped reflecting light, neither one would receive glory. If we are to receive glory for what we do, it must be for doing what we were created to do".

In the 1970's, a little known Episcopal Church in Darien, Ct decided to get their Vestry together and come up with a Mission Statement. It took some time but they settled on a very short but profound statement. Their Mission Statement would be, "To know Him and to make Him known"; however, it is easier said then done.

From the book of Joshua, we read of the story of Rehab who hides the two spies sent out by Joshua. She tells the two spies what is happening in the land where she is living.

She said to the men, *"I know that the Lord has given you the land, that the terror of you has fallen on us, and that all the inhabitants of the land are fainthearted because of you. For WE HAVE HEARD how the Lord dried up the water of the Red Sea for you when you came out of Egypt, and what you did to the two kings of the Amorites who were on the other side of the Jordan, Sihon and Og, whom you utterly destroyed. And AS SOON AS WE HEARD these things, our hearts melted; neither did there remain any more courage in anyone because of you, for the Lord your God, He is God in heaven above and on earth beneath. Josh 2:9-12 Emphasis author's*

In the Old Testament, God was making His name known by His Mighty Acts. His acts revealed His heart. All the Nation of Israel had to do was proclaim them among the peoples of the Earth.

The continuation of His mighty acts was, of course, conditional on their keeping the covenant. They were to keep His laws, walk in righteousness before Him and worship Him as prearranged by Moses and the Lord Himself.

If we are to claim our "Promised Land", what Mighty Acts are we proclaiming to the peoples of the Earth today? Do we have any memorial stones on display so that when our children ask us,

"What are these stones here for?", we can tell them what God did on our behalf?

Are we leading people to the Lord that they might be reconciled to the Father? Are we fighting evil spirits that hold other Christians in bondage mentally, psychologically, and either physically or spiritually? Are we just leaving everything up to God (saying He is in Control) or are **we** speaking to the wind to stop, the water to be turned into wine, and loafs and fishes to be multiplied? Are we expecting signs and wonders to be done in our midst? Are we casting out demons, setting the captives free?

Are our "God stories"; stories of His great and mighty acts, someone else's stories or are they our stories? These mighty acts of God show forth not only His wondrous power but also His compassion and goodness. God is a God of love and all His power is brought forth to reveal that great love.

We are commissioned to invade the enemy' kingdom and it will not be an easy fight. Nevertheless, it is time for us to take Dominion and proclaim the mighty Name of the Lord Jesus Christ to the peoples of the Earth.

How do we wage war against Satan?

Paul gives us these instructions in Eph 6:10-18

"Finally, my brethren, be strong in the Lord and in the power of His might. Put on the whole armor of God, that you may be able to stand against the wiles of the devil. For we do not wrestle against flesh and blood, but against principalities, against powers, against the rulers of the darkness of this age, against spiritual hosts of wickedness in the heavenly places. Therefore take up the whole armor of God, that you may be able to withstand in the evil day, and having done all, to stand.

Stand therefore, having girded your waist with truth, having put on the breastplate of righteousness, and having shod your feet with the preparation of the gospel of peace; above all, taking the shield of faith with which you will be able to quench all the fiery darts of the wicked one. And take the helmet of salvation, and the sword of the Spirit, which is the word of God; praying always with all prayer and supplication in the Spirit, being watchful to this end with all perseverance and supplication for all the saints"

The problem arises when we consider the method in which we wage this war. Some believe that God is in total control, therefore, all evil in this world is allowed and God will use it for His Glory. They believe all that happens has a purpose and they need to find out that purpose for themselves. They pray that God will give them wisdom to deal with every situation. Does this fit the definition of warfare?

In war, there is conflict, and fighting. There is a winner and a loser. The loser in the end loses something; gives up something. The winner does not ask; he demands. As soldiers in the Lord's Army, the Spirit tells us to take up the FULL armor of God. This is not a request; it is a command! We are to win this war. There is much at stake.

Paul talks of Epaphroditus, a fellow **soldier** (Phil2:25); Paul exhorts Timothy to endure hardship as a good **soldier** of Jesus Christ (2 Tim 2:3); and he addresses Apphia Archippus, our fellow **soldier** (Philemon 2:2).

Jesus spent much of His Earthly ministry engaging the enemy. He commanded Demons to come out and He healed the sick. Jesus has all authority and calls you to be His ambassador, an ambassador of the King. You have His authority therefore, to continue his work. You can take Dominion over the powers of darkness.

Mark 16:14-18

"Later He appeared to the eleven as they sat at the table; and He rebuked their unbelief and hardness of heart, because they did not believe those who had seen Him after He had risen. And He said to them, "Go into all the world and preach the gospel to every creature. He who believes and is baptized will be saved; but he who does not believe will be condemned. And these signs will follow those who believe: In My name they will cast out demons; they will speak with new tongues; they will take up serpents; and if they drink anything deadly, it will by no means hurt them; they will lay hands on the sick, and they will recover."

146

Chapter 9
Master Builders

Before Jesus left this Earth, He put everything in order so that His Father's Kingdom could grow in numbers as well as in maturity. His Church is to be the instrument to extend the Father's kingdom and making sure of its success was His responsibility. His Father has made Him His Lord and Christ and therefore, His final goal is to turn over all the kingdoms of this Earth, with all their authority and power, to His Father.

He set in place a structure of authority. We have already set out in understandable terms the fact that Jesus was under authority. He did nothing without His Father's permission. All too often, we are inclined to think or be affected by something that is of this world rather than by the Word of God. We think of authority as hierarchical and therefore the one at the top is superior over the ones below. This is not the case regarding relationships between the Godhead nor is it to be in the structure Jesus set up for building His Church.

Jesus set in place gifts to His Church. His gifts were not things, but men. Men who had been transformed by the very processes as outlined in this book. The Word of God that worked within them changed the thinking and the hearts of these men. Their spirits were strengthened with might through His Spirit in the inner man. Peter gives insight in how this happened and gives encouragement to us today.

He writes in *2 Peter 1:2-4, "Grace and peace be multiplied to you in the knowledge of God and of Jesus our Lord, as His divine power has given to us all things that pertain to life and godliness, through the knowledge of Him who called us by glory and virtue, by which have been given to us exceedingly great and precious promises, that through these you may be partakers of the divine nature, having escaped the corruption that is in the world through lust".*

What an awesome statement; that we through knowledge, divine power, and exceedingly great and precious promises, may be partakers of God's divine nature. This is how these men and women, which were part of the five-fold ministry as given in Ephesians 4:11 were able to carry out their tasks.

The Ministry of the Word

This is a very important topic for us to consider before we discuss the five-fold Ministry. It is important because God's Word comes through man. We have the Bible –the Word of God- but unless someone preaches the Word, how will the unbeliever know the way of salvation and God's Grand Plan. Without the Ministry of the Word, there is no work. God, from the beginning of time "said" and the work was done.

In the Old Testament, God spoke through a person(s), the Prophet(s). The Word came to them and they spoke what was given. They did not add their own thoughts, feelings or opinions. If they had added their humanness to what they were given, it would have ceased to be God's Word.

A change came however, when Jesus appeared in the incarnation. Here is the difference; God again uses a person but the person of Jesus is the Word. The Word was righteous, holy, and full of wisdom. In the Old Testament God merely uses a man's voice and personality but in Jesus; human feeling, thought and opinion were expressed as one in the same. Moreover, they were the same, because His feelings, thoughts and opinions were the same as God's.

In Jesus, God's revelation of Himself to man became a man. Jesus is the express image of His Father and what He speaks and does is the same as what His Father would say and do. We pointed out earlier in this book that in Matt 5:21 Jesus said, *"You have*

148

*heard that it was said to **those of old***", But Jesus now says, "*I say to you*". We must understand this profound difference. The first came from the prophets who spoke as they were instructed and spoke nothing more than they were given to speak. Jesus, however, speaks with authority, using His own feelings, thoughts and opinions. Through Jesus, the Father is getting closer to the fulfillment of His desire regarding the working of His Word.

The Father's intention is for man to be so radically transformed that Christ is completely formed in him. When he (man) speaks, he then would speak as an oracle of God. Those that minister the Word are to be so transformed. Here is the significant difference between Jesus and those God has ordained to minister the Word: When we consider Jesus, the Word of God made flesh; the Word came first and then was clothed with flesh. When we consider man, man came first and the flesh must be made to reveal the Word. His thoughts, feelings, opinions and actions must become the same as God's. What we have discussed in this book and more so in *BORN TO RULE*, is the process of Transformation that brings about God's image being formed in man; man becoming as living letters to be read by all men.

The Apostle Paul understood the need for spiritual revelation of Christ. He wrote, "*The eyes of your understanding being enlightened that ye may know what is the hope of his calling, and what the riches of the glory of his inheritance in the saints and what is the exceeding greatness of his power to us-ward who believe, according to the working of his mighty power which he wrought in Christ when he raised him from the dead and set him at his own right hand in the heavenly places far above all principality and power, and might, and dominion, and every name that is named, not only in this world, but also in that which is to come: And hath put all things under his feet, and gave him to be the head over all things to the Church". (Ephesians 1:18-21.*

THE FIVE-FOLD MINISTRY

The principle that controls the Word is this; the Word is to be seen and touched by man. It must influence Man in all that he thinks and does. The men and women involved in the five-fold ministry are those that are so transformed by the Word; that that which they speak is coming from God himself.

In BORN TO RULE, we described the transformation process by which we can judge those that claim to be Apostles, Prophets, Evangelist, Pastors and Teachers. The plain and simple truth is; if they do not measure up – don't listen to them.

The five-fold Ministry is as important today as it was in the 1st Century. However, whatever we call it, it is not as important as the task or function it is to perform. As with the Laying on of Hands, casting out demons, healing the sick; the five-fold ministry of Apostles, Prophets, Evangelist, Pastors and Teachers has been lost until recently. It is vital to the strengthening of every local church and Believer. It is also important to you as a minister of the Gospel of the Kingdom and as an individual that wants to make a difference with their life.

Much of the misunderstanding regarding the five-fold ministry is the direct result of Satan protecting his kingdom. The Church of the Lord Jesus Christ has the authority to pull down the strongholds of his kingdom therefore; Satan will do anything to prevent the Church from re-establishing the Kingdom of God in the hearts of men.

Jesus gave the Five-fold ministry to His Church in order that it might equip the Saints for the work of ministry and for their edifying until they all come to the unity of the faith in the knowledge of the Son of God. The Church is to bring each member unto a perfect man, to the measure of the stature of the fullness of Christ; that they should no longer be children, tossed back and forth and carried about with every wind of doctrine.

The job description for the five—fold ministry in general is this: prepare the Saints to catch the Wind of the Holy Spirit. A good way to describe the five-fold ministry is like what happens when you go to an optometrist to have your eyes checked for glasses. He first puts one lens into the machine so you can see the big picture and he then adds additional lens so you can progressively see clearer and clearer. So it is with the five-fold ministry.

The Apostle lays the first layer that reveals the big picture. The prophet comes along and lays down a layer that adds clarity regarding his function or task that the Lord has given him. The evangelist does the same and so on for the Pastor and Teacher. Just as you must have all the lenses in place to see clearly in the physical realm, we must have the complete five-fold ministry team involved in our lives in order to see clearly the full purpose and intent of the Lord in the spiritual realm.

The importance of the Five-Fold Ministry is similar to the need for two parents. Each brings to the child different and very important training.

Each leader must realize that, by himself, he is insufficient to bring about the maturity of the Saints. No leader can provide all the gifts and ministries that the people need that are under his care.

What we find in today's modern churches is that there are Pastors trying to do the task of two or three members of the five-fold ministry. They are the Evangelist, the Teacher and the Prophet all rolled into one. They are the lone single voice heard by the adherents or members. Some Pastors should be evangelist and others should be prophets but because the "Church at large" does not recognize these gifts, they are stuck where they are.

We must point out that even those involved in the five-fold ministry need the ministry of each other. They too are part of the body of Christ and each part of the body cannot exist by itself. The head cannot say it has no need of the toe.

Here's the point. When the Church only hears one voice, it is the voice of the grace given to that man. If a man is called by God to be an Evangelist then his calling (grace) will flavor every thing he preaches. If he is called to be a Pastor, then his calling will flavor every thing he preaches. If the Apostle does all the preaching, then his calling will flavor everything he preaches.

Here's the problem: the Church does not understand the differences between the gifts and therefore follows the man in the pulpit as if "this is all there is".

Some pastors feel that they need to protect "their" sheep or they feel they don't need anyone else to help them build their church. Jesus said, "I will build my Church" and I will give gifts of men to accomplish it because that is the only way to build my Church. Jesus will build His Church because His Church is built on the revelation of Himself.

To accomplish our purpose we must understand the mission of Christ; then we will be able to understand our calling. When we do, we understand what He meant when He said, "I will build my Church and the gates of hell shall not prevail against it." The gates of hell refer to spiritual opposition by demonic government. As Christians, you and I are involved in a spiritual war for dominion.

Without the five-fold ministry, the Church will not hear the whole story or see the complete picture. The Church will be fed but the diet will be insufficient and the body will be weak. The tree leans in the direction of the sun. If the Church only hears one voice, it will lean in that direction and the Church becomes departmentalized and will develop its own culture.

We make much commotion over the fact that each local church is sovereign or self-governing. With this sovereignty comes the freedom to accept Scripture as the local pastor and church board intercepts it. They can organize how they conduct their worship service, their educational programs and whatever else they involve themselves. There are many examples of non-uniformity among churches that we all respect. Nevertheless, I respectfully submit that without the oversight of the five-fold ministry the Church has lost its faithfulness to the mandate given by Christ himself; that of preaching the Gospel of the Kingdom of God. By rejecting the five-fold ministry, they have rejected Christ himself, who said that He would build His Church.

It is not the intent of this author to bring a treatise on the subject of the five-fold ministry, but we must understand their importance and their function in order to appreciate the wisdom of our Lord. We will begin by explaining each function as it pertains to building up the body of Christ.

There is no need to go over again the preparation for ministry, as it is the same for those men involved in the five-fold offices under consideration. Each of the positions involve Leadership and Leadership is influence. You influence others for good or for bad. Although that sounds simple, it is more complicated than most people think. Everyone from the bully on the playground to the Apostle influence someone. The goal or purpose of that influence is what we want to consider next.

Some general comments regarding all those involved in the five-fold ministry - a true Apostle, Prophet, Evangelist, Pastor and Teacher knows that he should not think more highly of himself than he ought to think. He also knows that every good and perfect gift comes from God. He knows that he is no better than his Master and as his Master came to serve, he too must be a servant. Humility of spirit is the key word for these men and women.

It is important to point out that many are given visions and are in positions of leadership but not all are called to be an Apostle. Many may have the gift of prophecy but not all are called to be a Prophet. All Believers are called to evangelize but not all are called to be an Evangelist. Many are called to pastor or to shepherd others but not all are called to the responsibility of Pastor. Many are called to teach but not all are called to the responsibility of Teacher.

There is a heavy responsibility and accountability for all who accept the Lord's call to one of these positions of leadership. One should weigh the consequences of their possible failure seriously before accepting the honor. One can take upon himself the title but one cannot take upon himself the honor or the glory for the fulfillment of the task given.

APOSTLE

The Apostle gets the most attention because we consider him the Leader or the one on the top rung of the ladder. His responsibility and accountability are the greatest therefore; we should make sure we cover him in prayer. Honor is given to whom honor is due –and this is right- but he is just a man like the rest of us.

If any one sees the big picture, it is the Apostle and he is responsible for sharing that with the rest of those that are part of his team. It is to the Apostle that God reveals the deep mysteries of the Kingdom. Therefore, all others of the apostolic team need to be in close contact with the Apostle, for these revelations will govern and direct their lives. These revelations will then in turn direct their ministry to the Saints.

Acceptance of apostolic authority is voluntary. Those churches that are part of a denomination will possibly reject such a suggestion. Those that are hungry for a move of God and are burdened for the re-establishment of the Kingdom of God; they will embrace this revelation and seek out Apostles to whom they can attach themselves. It may be that their Bishop, superintendent, or sectional presbyter is the Apostle, clothed as a Pastor.

The Apostolic Gift will make room for itself. The Spirit of God will cause others to recognize the Gift and the authority and Spiritual Gifts that accompany it.

The following is what others might see working in an Apostle:

A Visionary – sees things as God sees them and has the ability to cast that vision so that others buy into it

A Burden for the lost that is revealed by his love and sacrificial living for all people

A Burden for the building up of the body of Christ by teaching truths that transform and empower

A concern for the members of Christ body; each fulfilling their purpose

A concern for righteousness and holiness in the Church that is not afraid to discipline

An ability to know the hearts of men and place them into positions of leadership

PROPHET

This might be the one gift given to the Church that is most abused. Because prophecy is thought of as insight into the future, many have prophesied falsely and because it sounds so godlike, it goes undiscovered as no one bothers to check it out. The Office of Prophet is more than foretelling, it is much deeper and broader than that.

The Prophet's function is a ministry of restoration through revelation. The Prophet must completely yield himself to the Holy Spirit, as his ministry is hard for the people to accept and therefore receives much opposition.

God, looking down from His vantage point and seeing that the Church is deviating from its course, brings about the ministry of the Prophet. Like a football coach whose team is playing terrible and losing games, he calls us back to basics, makes a re-pronouncement of God's purpose and thoughts. God is foremost interested in the fulfilling His purpose through His people and the Prophet keeps that before the people.

Like individuals, the Church can and does, become sidetracked and then begin to emphasis the part instead of the whole. The Prophet recognizes that Purpose governs everything. His function is to present God's full, original and complete purpose according to the Mind of God. Like Moses, whose business it was to be exact in every detail of the tabernacle, the Prophet brings all the details before the Church in order that God's purpose will unfold exactly as His thoughts presented it.

The Prophet does not occupy an office in a Church, He is not a professional, trained and qualified (even though he may be in full time ministry); he is a man of God who must come to God repeatedly to receive revelation. As he comes before God, the Holy Spirit speaks and spiritual things become fresh, alive and full of energy. The Prophet speaks only when he has something to say because it is the anointing that makes his words come alive, because they are coming from the living God.

This gift, given by Christ to the Church, is extremely important. To dismiss this gift as part of the ancient past is to deprive the Church of a voice that reveals truths hidden in Scripture that relate to the present day. Many Scriptures are not just for one period in history but are also for others. There were prophecies about Jesus, written thousands of years before He was born, that had meaning also for the day in which they were spoken. Just as in the days of the Old Testament, The Holy Spirit is unveiling the meaning of Scripture for us today through His Prophets.

This is a hard truth to swallow, but the majority of Pastors today are just being echoes of preachers from another generation. They read what others have said in commentaries and books about a certain Scripture and then repeat it as if it was their own. There is nothing wrong with repeating others and being an echo, if we are receiving the same revelation that has come from our own study and from our relationship with the Holy Spirit.

As the Prophet brings light to Scriptures that have been in darkness until the present hour, Pastors and Teachers can now expound on these truths for the body of Christ. God can never be satisfied with anything less than the image of His son being formed in and then represented by His Church.

The following is what others might see working in a Prophet:

A burden for the truth of the Scripture – the prophet is concerned with bringing the spiritual implications of things before the citizens of the Kingdom. His burden is for them to have understanding of the significance of things in their spiritual value and meaning.

A burden for righteousness and holiness in the land with fearlessness in the fulfilling of his commission to speak for his king, even in the face of death

A Man of Prayer – Before he speaks, he spends time with God, allowing Him to see what God sees. It is only as he is in His presence does the revelation and the anointing come to him. He stands in the gap interceding and then as he hears from

God he makes the pronouncement of judgment. His concern is for the people and as such, he is on the lookout for the approaching enemy and is ready to speak forth to those of influence to sound the alarm. A Prophet knows the mind of Christ, his king and is not afraid to let it be known.

Prophets benefit the Body of Christ by announcing, activating, imparting, confirming, and unlocking various times and seasons in Believers' lives.

EVANGELIST

The Evangelist has fallen out of favor in recent years because of bad conduct by a few. The Pastor, who is the one who invites the Evangelist to come to their church, has never really understood their place in the five-fold ministry. Often the Evangelist is looked upon as one who unravels the cord that the Pastor has been weaving and then goes off, leaving the Pastor to pick up the threads. This is often true because the true Evangelist is in contact with the Apostle or Prophet and has received revelation that the Pastor does not have. Sadly, in years past, Evangelists were looking to build their own ministry.

The Evangelist is there to stir up the people (including the Pastor) to reach those who are under the domain of the evil one. He is there to awaken the Church to the power of the Gospel of the Kingdom, as seen when Jesus authenticates the ministry by signs and wonders that follow. For those that have not been Baptized in the Holy Spirit, he is there to stir up their spirit and prepare then for the task placed before them. The Gifts of the Spirit are in operation to make known the greatness of our God and that encourages the people to bring in their friends, family, coworkers and others to the meetings.

The Evangelist is part of the five-fold ministry team and therefore he is in contact with the Apostle and the Prophet. His ministry adds to the work that they are already doing in laying the foundation for kingdom ministry. Without his ministry, the people grow weak and lose their zeal for going out to deliver the captives and bring them into the kingdom. The people begin to rely on advertizing, the programs, the building and the great preaching of their pastor to bring the sinners into the kingdom.

The Church begins to lose its influence when the people lose the joy that comes to them when a sinner is saved. The Church becomes introverted and then is concerned with the blessings of the Lord instead of His Grand Plan for His people.

This is what we might see in working in the Evangelist:

A burden for those that are under the control of the Devil

A burden for the Church that has lost its desire to make the name of the Lord known

A desire to teach and train the Saints to go out into the highways and byways to reach those not in the kingdom

He brings a message that captures the heart of God's people that excites them to turn their world upside down, to influence their culture and return the culture of the kingdom of God to where they live.

PASTOR

The Pastor, in today's society, is the main man of influence in the Church. Everything rest and falls on what he does and says. His every word is taken as truth and that should weigh heavily on his heart.

We find the Pastor doing all those things that we normally consider them to do like: performing marriages, water baptisms, funerals, counseling those in trouble, preaching and the regular administrative duties that are required.

The REAL responsibility for the Pastor is teaching the culture of the Kingdom. Kingdom Culture is so different from the world's culture that without the Pastor's influence, families will be vulnerable to accept another culture, the culture of the World. Families are exposed to the world's culture at work, school, TV, sport events, from friends, family members and even in some so-called Christian churches.

We look upon the Pastor as the Shepherd. He is to instill a faith into the sheep so that they know that all their needs will be met because the Good Shepherd loves them. Like a shepherd, he is to lead the sheep to quiet waters and green pastures. He is to feed them the Word of God that they might grow up into Christ. He is to take them to fields where they can lay down and find peace. He is to be on guard and be ready to protect them from their enemies. He is to make it possible for them not to be afraid, even in the mist of evil and turmoil.

He helps his people to have an encounter with their God that causes their faith to increase in order to make His Name known. He is to preach in such a way that the people develop a thirst and hunger for Righteousness. For, righteousness distinguishes the Kingdom of God.

This is what we might see in working in the Pastor:

His biggest responsibility is to help his people work out their salvation so that Christ is formed in them. Sheep are prone to stray and wander; therefore, the Pastor must continually bring before them the consequences of sin.

He makes himself available for the people in his church.

The focal point of his ministry is the preaching on topics regarding everyday living such as: Mercy, Grace, Repentance, Holiness, Love, Marriage, Forgiveness, Humility, Relationships, Tithing, Physical Healing and Deliverance.

He makes the ministry of the Apostle, Prophet, Evangelist and Teacher available to his people.

He involves his people in missions, feeding the poor, providing for the homeless, helping those in drug programs, and ministering to those in prison. One does not learn to serve without serving or to give without giving.

The Pastor keeps the history of the people of God before them. Without a knowledge of their past, they will not know how they got where they are or if they are on track to where they are going.

TEACHER

The Teacher works closely with the Pastor. He may have his own radio or TV ministry but he is accountable to the others in the five-fold ministry. Where he often goes astray is when he begins to align himself with a certain line of thought and it produces a following. He is then guilty of using his gift as a means of satisfying the flesh instead of bringing his audience to fulfill the purposes and intent of God.

The teacher has been given insight and wisdom to bring to the people. The meaning of scriptures, so that they clearly understand, is his to give. He makes Scripture applicable to their every day life so they can exhibit God's grace in their activities, whether family, work, social and even private.

Teachers must be careful of what they teach, as they are trusted as having insight that few have. *"My brethren, let not many of you become teachers, knowing that we shall receive a stricter judgment. For we all stumble in many things. If anyone does not stumble in word, he is a perfect man, able also to bridle the whole body. Indeed, we put bits in horses' mouths that they may obey us, and we turn their whole body. Look also at ships: although they are so large and are driven by fierce winds, they are turned by a very small rudder wherever the pilot desires. Even so the tongue is a little member and boasts great things". James 3:1-5*

The teacher must not only be a student of the Word but must wait upon the Holy Spirit in order to fit all the pieces of the puzzle together; seeing clearly the meaning of the subject matter. He has been given wisdom and understanding but he cannot rely upon solely his mind. He too lives in this world and is susceptible to the deceit of the Devil. He must be on guard at all times.

This is what we might see in working in the Teacher:

A burden for the people to walk in the truth of the Word

A dedication to study to make himself approved and helping others to do likewise

A student of presentation; making all things understandable to all, no matter their education, social or economic standing, mental capability, or age

Worksheet to Receiving FAITH

Date and Circle the specific Scripture
When you receive Hope and again for Faith

List ALL Scriptures that lead to the fulfillment of your desire	Write your need

About the Author
Robert Farrier

Robert Farrier, founder of Kingdom Connections, travels internationally proclaiming the gospel of the Kingdom and awakening God's people to the wonder of Living in the Kingdom.

He is a product of the Charismatic movement and since that time he has held strong to the belief that the Word of God is the standard by which all things are to be judged. He has remembered a saying he learned from his pastor long ago, "If you guide your life by just the Word you will dry up. If you guide your life by just the Spirit you will blow up. If you allow the Spirit to guide your life by the Word, you will grow up." Therefore, he has held to a balance of the Word and the Spirit.

Robert graduated from Southeastern University in 1979. He went on pastor in Vermont and New York. Later, as Director of Education in a large Church in Upstate New York, Robert's interests in mentoring the saints in the fulfilling of God's Grand Plan began to emerge.

In the last 20 years Robert has traveled overseas to the underdeveloped nations holding Pastor Conferences to awaken within them a vision of the Kingdom of God. He shares the principles that he learned in his daily walk with the Lord regarding the leading of the Spirit that produces lasting results. Robert continues his ministry today to the nations of the world with an emphasis in Haiti.

The revelation of the principles of Transformation and Empowerment are now incorporated in the teaching and preaching ministry of Kingdom Connections, Inc, a non-profit ministry. For several years Robert has been teaching the material that is now found in two of his books, *"BORN TO RULE" and "A KNIGDOM WHICH CANNOT BE SHAKEN"*.

Robert draws on his 38 years of walking with the Lord, his experience as a Pastor, Missionary/Evangelist, and Teacher.

He is available for weekend Seminars and Pastor's Conferences.

You can contact Bob through his blog by going to his web page and clicking of the blog tab
OR
bob@kingdomfaithconnection.com

Please check out the Kingdom Connections website:
www.kingdomfaithconnection.com

www.ingramcontent.com/pod-product-compliance
Lightning Source LLC
Chambersburg PA
CBHW051837090426

42736CB00011B/1849